MINDFULNESS

An Hachette UK Company
www.hachette.co.uk

First published in Great Britain in 2021 by
Godsfield, an imprint of
Octopus Publishing Group Ltd
Carmelite House
50 Victoria Embankment
London EC4Y 0DZ
www.octopusbooks.co.uk
www.octopusbooksusa.com

Distributed in the US by
Hachette Book Group
1290 Avenue of the Americas
4th and 5th Floors
New York, NY 10104

Distributed in Canada by
Canadian Manda Group
664 Annette St.
Toronto, Ontario, Canada M6S 2C8

ISBN 978-1-84181-498-8

A CIP catalogue record for this book is available
from the British Library.

Printed and bound in China

10 9 8 7 6 5 4 3 2 1

All reasonable care has been taken in the
preparation of this book but the information
it contains is not intended to take the place of
treatment by a qualified medical practitioner.

Before making any changes in your health
regime, always consult a doctor. While
all the therapies detailed in this book are
completely safe if done correctly, you must
seek professional advice if you are in any doubt
about any medical condition. Any application
of the ideas and information contained in this
book is at the reader's sole discretion and risk.

Publishing Director: Stephanie Jackson
Art Director: Yasia Williams-Leedham
Production Controller: Serena Savini

Project Editor: Clare Churly
Copy-editor: Mandy Greenfield
Designer: Leonardo Collina
Illustrator: Emilia Franchini

MINDFULNESS

THE GUIDE TO PRINCIPLES, PRACTICES AND MORE

Dr Patrizia Collard

Contents

Introduction

The art of being with "what is" – the ability to be mindful – is perhaps more important than ever before in these changing times. With mindfulness we can truly help ourselves, even when we are alone, to remain strong, reduce fear, find our focus and discover moments of joy. If we can manage to meditate for even as little as ten minutes a day, if we can truly enjoy the meals that many of us are able to consume, if we can look out of the open window, breathe in the fresh air, look at the sky, the clouds, hear the birdsong and other sounds of life, feel the rays of the sun or the splatter of rain, the touch of wind, the smells that are offered freely, if we can sing songs out of our open windows … if all of this is accessible to us, then we can create moments of pleasure within ourselves, purpose in each in- and out-breath we take, and reasons for being alive!

The recent pandemic has brought about a reconnection to nature: local woodlands, parks, riversides and beaches. This is our rebirth, a new emerging consciousness that recognizes our intrinsic closeness to nature and what it can teach us about being present in our lives when there is instability around us.

I became most deeply aware of the fine line we must not cross if we wish our planet to survive while watching David Attenborough's film *A Life on Our Planet*. In this beautiful yet unsettling documentary he declares himself to be a 93-year-old witness who has been observing the miracles of nature for more than 60 years. And it is with great sadness that he shares how humankind has taken over the wilderness, the savannahs, the seas, the great woodlands and the rainforests. He states without shame how we have blindly exploited planet Earth and explains that if we want her to recover – and yes, there is still a chance – we need to change drastically! In fact, Attenborough is so outspoken that I remember some of his invitations by heart, like, for example, changing to a mainly plant-based diet. He emphasizes that only if we care for nature, will she care for us. And thus, I perceive mindfulness and compassion to empower us not only to benefit ourselves but all living things.

It is my deep hope that this companion to mindfulness will help you find your feet, and your passion, in this new way of being alive.

How Mindfulness Changed My Life

My original training was in stress-coaching, a diploma that incorporated many skills akin to meditation, such as relaxation, self-hypnosis, visualization and affirmations. A long stay in the Far East also offered me the opportunity to study Tai Chi, Chi Gong, yoga and meditation. Furthermore, for as long as I can remember I had a desire to understand creation and all "that is", and despite the fact that nobody in my family prayed or believed in anything, I started to attend Christian services from the age of six years onward. This became another foundation of my personal awareness and compassion.

My first degree in literature and the Arts from Oxford helped me to understand the art of writing more deeply, so I did not experience any inhibitions toward the written word, and to date I have published 12 books and many academic papers. In my late twenties (after a few years of focusing mainly on motherhood) I was able to complete my PhD and numerous theses for diplomas in psychotherapy, including Cognitive Behavioural Therapy (CBT), Multimodal Therapy, Rational Emotive Behaviour Therapy and drug and alcohol studies. By the time I ventured into my personal discovery of Eastern philosophies (mindfulness, yoga, Buddhism and Taoism) I had a wide knowledge base to draw on, to which I could connect my new insights.

Upon returning to London from Beijing in 2000, I started studying Mindfulness-Based Stress Reduction (MBSR) and Mindfulness-Based Cognitive Therapy (MBCT). While I had been far away developing my own yoga and meditation practice, mindfulness had found its way into medicine and Cognitive Behavioural Psychotherapy. In 2001 I founded Entermindfulness, which is an expansion of my original company Stressminus, which I created in the 1990s.

It was a cumbersome journey to meet the scientist and meditation teacher Jon Kabat-Zinn (I trained for six week-long intensive courses with him in Europe), and I bumped into him again in 2005 in Gothenburg at a conference called "Making Sense of the 21st Century". This conference was a pivotal moment for me, because it was there that I realized my calling was to move more closely into the development of MBCT for the general public, rather than working solely with a clinical population or with university trainees in psychotherapy.

I completed my teacher development in Mindfulness-based Interventions at Bangor University. Although I am an accredited cognitive behavioural therapist, I felt drawn to offer Mindfulness-Based Cognitive Training for stress reduction to the general public. I also co-founded an Austrian organization called Achtsamkeit Leben (Living

Mindfulness) and brought together the best of MBSR and MBCT in courses that helped people to deal with stress, low mood, fear and other destructive emotions. This was how mindfulness changed my life and continues to direct it today.

How to Use This Guide

Each chapter in this book can be read and processed on its own. If one theme interests you more than others, you can read ahead, but if you are new to mindfulness I would suggest that you really focus on the first few chapters, and in particular on A Mindful Day (see pages 46–77), which includes several short meditations. It will help you develop your own "everyday practice" and become familiar with meditative skills. Please reread this chapter regularly (maybe once a week or once a month) and simultaneously try keeping a journal, monitoring step-by-step how mindfulness neuropathways (connected nerves along which electrical impulses travel) are growing and affecting your day-to-day behaviour and wellbeing.

If you are already practising mindfulness meditation, you may find the chapters on relationships and mental wellbeing particularly useful. Even if you simply intend to deepen your own practice, the chapter entitled A Mindfulness Journey, Week by Week (see page 250) offers insights into how to work with certain meditations more deeply, how to use them to cope with life's challenges, and other aspects of mindfulness that the very committed student will hopefully consider enlightening.

Each chapter includes poetry to support the theme in question. I feel strongly that poems can help us develop a sense of being fully present, and can engage us in sustained attention. Kindly read each poem at the end of the chapter and then sit with it. Maybe read it more than once, and see whether it helps to deepen the insights offered in the text.

Directory of Meditations and Mindfulness Practices

Practice	Duration	Page
Body Scan (1)	30–40 minutes	page 196
Body Scan (2)	10–15 minutes	page 254
Breathing In for Me, Breathing Out for You	20 minutes	page 214
Connecting with Loss	20–25 minutes	page 208
Going for a Mindful Walk	at least 10 minutes	page 211
Guided Walking Journey	10–15 minutes	page 110
Invoking Joy Meditation	5–10 minutes	page 226
Lake Meditation	5 minutes	page 125
Loving-kindness (*Metta*) Meditation	10–15 minutes	page 170
Meditation to Reduce Cravings	10–15 minutes	page 157
Mindful Breathing	5–10 minutes	page 50
Mindful Minute	a few minutes	page 257
Mindful Self-compassion Break	5 minutes	page 212
Mindful "Soften/Soothe/Allow" Meditation	15–20 minutes	page 140
Mindful Walking (1)	10–20 minutes	page 108
Mindful Walking (2)	10–20 minutes	page 270
Mindful Yoga	20 minutes	page 244
Mindfulness Wheel	5–10 minutes	page 277

Directory of Meditations and Mindfulness Practices

Practice	Duration	Page
Mountain Meditation	5 minutes	page 124
Mountain Pose	about 5 minutes	page 122
Mountain Pose with Arms Up	about 5 minutes	page 123
Pleasant-event Diary	5–20 minutes	page 120
Raisin Exercise	5 minutes	page 64
Self-compassion Writing	20 minutes	page 240
Simple Sun Salutation	12–15 minutes	page 54
Sitting with Your Thoughts (1)	15–20 minutes	page 118
Sitting with Your Thoughts (2)	10–15 minutes	page 262
Sleep Meditation	15 minutes	page 169
Spinal Rotation	5–10 minutes	page 268
Three-step Breathing Space (1)	3–5 minutes	page 68
Three-step Breathing Space (2)	3–5 minutes	page 274
Upright Body Scan	5–10 minutes	page 200
Viewing Mindfulness	10 minutes	page 190
When Big Feelings Are Present Meditation	10 minutes	page 92
Yoga to Find Your Centre	at least 20 minutes	page 246

How to Approach the Mindfulness Practices

Starting any new activity or practice can be daunting, especially if it is something that you have never tried before. Luckily, to start living more mindfully you don't need any prior knowledge, special clothing or expensive equipment. All you need is a desire to change.

Essentially, mindfulness is about living in the moment without judgement and accepting as best as you can "what is": the pleasant, the difficult and that which is simply neutral. The mindfulness practices in this book can help you find more balance and a sense of acceptance for whatever life presents you with at any given moment. There is no right or wrong way to becoming more mindful; your connection with this new "you" will grow organically. However, there are some things you can do to make your mindfulness journey go more smoothly.

Find a Regular Space at Home to Practice

Choosing a particular spot at home for your mindfulness practice will help your subconscious to connect this space with feelings of peace and stillness. If you have a spare room with a favourite chair for seated exercises, or space on the floor for a yoga mat for lying down, that is wonderful. But not everyone has this extra room – so instead you may choose to use your bedroom or your living room; where is not important, you just need to feel comfortable. However, I would avoid rooms where you work because they can be unconsciously connected to "job" activities and you may find it more challenging to switch off.

Furthermore, it could be useful to gather together a few props to help you feel comfortable: you may wish to have a warm blanket to hand; if you want to lie on the floor some cushions to support your head or back will be helpful; and a candle or a beautiful stone can be used to settle the active mind. Finally, it can be a good idea to dim the lights when you are practising mindfulness – this will send a message to your subconscious that you are slowing down and taking time to connect with your inner self.

Buy a Mindfulness Journal

Writing a journal will help you to keep a record of your experiences, and it can be an important tool for tracking your voyage and transformation. It will serve as a wonderful reminder of your journey into mindfulness. Kindly be inspired when you select your journal; choose one in a colour you love or decorate the cover with photos, stickers or even dried flowers to create something that in itself is a piece of mindfulness.

How often should you journal? It is up to you; you may write a little or a lot. But when you do write, note down your feelings, your reactions to the exercises, how you experienced them and anything else you feel is important. Even writing itself can become a mindful activity: jot down why you want to be mindful in that moment (including why you long for more mindful awareness into your life). You can also use your journal to set an intention of when you want to "be mindful" during a regular daily activity (walking the dog, washing up, hanging out the washing — whatever suits you). Alternatively, you may wish to set a time and day for a more formal, meditative practice — again note this down in your Mindfulness Journal. Even if you start with writing for just five minutes a day, a journal is the perfect way to support your mindfulness journey.

Read the Practices First and Record Them for Playback

Please do take your time and do not rush when reading this book or practising a meditation. Apply mindfulness at every step of your journey! Simply be, moment by moment, step by step.

Kindly read through any exercise first, let it sink in and then gently start practising. You may find it helpful to read them aloud slowly — this way you can clarify any instructions beforehand. If appropriate, you may also wish to record yourself reading a particular exercise aloud (using your mobile phone). You can play this recording back as you do the exercise — this will help you to fully immerse yourself in the mindfulness practice without having to keep checking this book for instructions.

Dealing with Disability

Some of the exercises ask you to stand, but you may find this position difficult for different reasons. Many of the practices, however, do give alternative options: you can sit, lie on the floor or relax in your bed in a prone position. What is important is that you feel comfortable, and safe, so use your knowledge of your body to pick a resting, meditative pose that is right for you.

When to Practise

You may choose to connect with your mindfulness practice early in the morning before you begin your day, perhaps setting time aside to do one of the ten-minute techniques. Due to family, animals and work commitments, though, this morning slot may not feel like it is possible for everyone. However, just spending a few moments connecting with the breath before you get out of bed, or mentally listing three things that you are grateful for (see Developing a Gratitude Practice, page 74) are mini-mindfulness practices that can set the right intention for the rest of your day.

As time progresses, mindfulness will become a natural way of being throughout your whole day. For example, you may find yourself doing a short mindfulness breath practice on the commute to work as a quick intervention when normally you would feel stressed. And, after a particularly hard day, you may wish to do the Body Scan (see page 196) to release stress and tension, even though you may have already completed some practice time that morning. But really, there is no good or bad time for mindfulness, just make it part of your everyday life.

Practice Techniques and Terms

Throughout this book, you may come across some unfamiliar terms. Here, I have outlined a few of the most important concepts of mindfulness to help you grasp the basics; as you progress through this book these ideas will become more familiar.

Anchoring

When you begin any meditative practice, it is natural for your mind to wander. Buddhist scholars would call this restlessness the "monkey mind" – describing the mind jumping from thought to thought like a monkey jumping around a tree. But there are simple ways to stop the mind wandering, to anchor yourself in the present. Connecting with the breath can be an effective and quick anchor. Alternatively, you may feel your sitting bones connected to the chair or your feet to the floor.

Attention

What do we mean by "attention"? For example, in the Body Scan (see page 196) you will be asked to bring attention to your feet, knees and so on. Some of you may visualize this body part, whereas I would like to encourage you to mentally bring awareness to it and sense or feel it as best as you can.

Points of Refuge

Your home should be your sanctuary, your safe haven, and as part of this journey you are going to create a special place (a refuge) in your home to practise your mindfulness exercises. In the wider world, there are other points of refuge where you can experience mindfulness: on a retreat, in a favourite wood or spot in nature, perhaps even at a close friend's home – enjoying the present moment in good company. See mindfulness as opening a door to refuge in your life – whatever form it takes.

Some Words of Caution

Mindfulness is a wonderful tool, but practising on your own may not be appropriate for everyone. If you suffer from any mental health issues, or you are feeling vulnerable or have recently experienced a bereavement, please find a properly trained teacher and study mindfulness meditation under supervision. Like any new skill, it takes patience and repetition in order to reap the rewards and change your mental and physical wellbeing and it is best to do this in a safe way.

Learn to Enjoy Life

You are about to take the first important steps on your mindfulness journey. Don't try to measure your "progress", mindfulness is all about "being" and not striving for goals. See this book as a guide, and an invitation, to enjoy your life through slowing down and appreciating the small things.

Enjoy!

Patrizia Collard

An Invitation to Unity and Love

From the oceans to the seas, to the rivers and the brooks
The love of life in the seas, upon the Earth, the land is purely rejoicing.
We celebrate the gift of living!
For *prana* is the notion to be rejoiced around the nations,
With movement of the mind to the blessings of the hearts,
With actions and intentions of kindness, the world can reunite in love,
Bringing soul-filled peace and harmony from the skies above to the core
of Mother Earth and beyond.
So enjoy these special moments to re-create our global world with peace
and harmony throughout the nations.
Breathe deep, breathe kindness, celebrate *prana*!

No matter what our surface differences may be — all elements of diversity —
We are all one, connected by source, with the blessings of Earth, Fire,
Water and AIR!
Each one of us has a responsibility to "BE" the best we can "BE".
Through all walks of life, wherever one may journey, we are all
connected as one!
Celebrate *prana*, celebrate life, rejoice in connectivity through
the passages of life!
Breathe deep, be strong, love well!

– Georgina Hunter, healer, holistic therapist and yoga practitioner[1]

1
AWAKENING TO MINDFULNESS

Mindfulness:
Spirit and Science

The ancient concept of learning awareness through the practice of
meditation has been discussed for thousands of years in Vedic and
Buddhist texts, and more recently in books and research papers
written by psychologists, psychotherapists and teachers of mindfulness
and compassion.

Siddhartha (the Buddha) decided early on in his life to learn more about
how to overcome suffering. First, he practised Shamata meditation (creating
a blissful state), but when he returned to normal life he still felt emotional
pain and observed misery. Thereafter he experimented with the yogis
(those who were proficient in yoga) who inhabited the woods. They
stood on one leg for hours, ate hardly anything (just bark from trees), and
Siddhartha experienced this practice as another form of suffering, rather
than as insight. So he started to look for the middle ground (Vipassana)
– a balanced approach, with no escape into suffering or bliss, but rather
observing life moment by moment as it unravels. Here he felt alert,
had more focus and was aware of his thoughts and feelings and able to
implement wise actions. By connecting with compassion for others he
eventually reached a sense of identity – he became "awakened".

Understanding Mindfulness

The Mind and Life Institute, which is based in Charlottesville, Virginia, aims to bridge science and contemplative wisdom, and to foster insight and inspire action toward flourishing, in order to better understand the mind and create positive change in the world.

Ever since the beginning of the institute, a group of highly reputable researchers has been meeting for one week each year to deepen our understanding of what happens in the brain and the body when we meditate. Numerous books and papers endorse what scientists have found out about the practice of mindfulness, and how scans show that the meditator's brain changes in certain areas to display a developed sense of peace and focus. As the Mind and Life Institute states:

> Our mission has evolved in response to a global crisis of disconnection: from loneliness and isolation to racism and tribalism, our disconnection from one another is causing tremendous suffering for people and the planet. We believe that this crisis starts in the human mind — and that the solution can start there, as well.[1]

I believe it is here that the true source of secular mindfulness can be found: at the meeting point of compassion and science, where scientific research and deep ancient wisdom can explore their common ground and share any important findings with the world at large.

Of course there were other pioneers who made invaluable contributions, such as Jon Kabat-Zinn. He initiated the Stress Reduction Clinic and the Center for Mindfulness in Medicine, Health Care and Society at the University of Massachusetts Medical School and started research into the effects of MBSR in the 1990s and has published more than 120 papers to date. (He defines mindfulness as a "radical act of love and sanity".[2]) But in the background the annual meetings between the researchers at the Mind and Life Institute laid the foundation for deepening the world's interest in mindfulness. If science can prove it, there must be something special to it! Slowly the world began to listen.

After approximately 25 years of research more and more evidence indicates that the regular, consistent practice of mindfulness leaves lasting physical traces in the brain; several neural networks can be enhanced, and some parts of the brain connect more deeply. The physician and wellbeing consultant Dr Parneet Pal says: "Buddhist monks whose brains get researched in labs … are Olympic champions … They have practised for more than sixty thousand hours. So, the sky's the limit … But I would say start small and build from there."[3]

This phenomenon is called neuroplasticity, and it is the astonishing capability of our brains to continue to change vigorously throughout our lives. And on top of that, there are a multitude of physical benefits that we can experience when integrating mindfulness into our daily life.

At this point it is important to emphasize, to avoid disappointment, that practising mindfulness will not lead directly to a state of regular blissfulness, relaxation and absolute peace – either in your individual life or on a global level. It's more about letting go of the goal of bliss (if you want it to happen, it might not) and seeing what arises. These states of being might be achieved through meditative practice, but they are not the only goal of mindfulness.

What I feel is most important at this point in human history is attempting to reach insight – with mindfulness offering us a deep "knowing and seeing" of what the actual moment we are experiencing right now is all about. We may thereby reach a deeper understanding of what needs to be done in a potentially dangerous situation – both for the planet at large, and on the micro–level as well. In addition we may become fully awake to the little gems of joy and beauty that life offers to us throughout our waking and sleeping hours.

By learning to slow down and live in the present moment – be it good, bad or neutral – we will deepen our experience of being alive here and now. We will comprehend that nothing lasts forever and that everything passes at last. Once we can really grasp this and commit to it, we may no longer strive for more power, more possessions. We may truly understand that *NOW* is all there is, and that this suffices.

Of course it is the human condition that triggers the attitude of holding on to all that we enjoy and love, and pushing away all that is unpleasant. But we can learn that the ever-changing patterns of being alive offer us different forms and shapes of experience: here now – gone later. This impermanence is true for every living organism.

And now you ask in your heart, "How shall we
distinguish that which is good in pleasure from that
which is not good?"
Go to your fields and your gardens, and you shall learn
that it is the pleasure of the bee to gather honey
of the flower,
But it is also the pleasure of the flower to yield its honey
to the bee.
For to the bee a flower is a fountain of life,
And to the flower a bee is a messenger of love,
And to both, bee and flower, the giving and the receiving
of pleasure is a need and an ecstasy.

People of Orphalese, be in your pleasures like the flowers
and the bees.

– Kahlil Gibran, Lebanese-American writer, poet,
visual artist and philosopher (1883–1931)[4]

Why We Need Mindfulness Now More Than Ever

"The education of attention would be an education par excellence."

— William James, American psychologist (1842–1910)

Does your mind wander? Mind-wandering happens when our thoughts run from one topic to the next — and it can be the cause of feelings of dissatisfaction. While some mind-wandering is normal, if we find ourselves in a constant maze of thoughts we can lose focus and motivation.

Research by Harvard psychologists Matthew A Killingsworth and Daniel T Gilbert) suggests that mindfulness can reduce mind-wandering.[1] Just imagine if you could get back at least one hour of your time a day by practising a short meditation. I believe it's worth ten minutes of daily practice to develop your mindfulness muscle and create new neuropathways.

Neuroimaging studies have demonstrated that mindfulness increases activation in the anterior cingulate cortex (ACC) of the brain, an area that is involved in decision-making and attention. Through better control of attention, it can become easier to focus on a present task, rather than being distracted by worries. Mindfulness practice is like a "workout" for the brain. The cortex becomes thicker, which improves long-term memory; our level of compassion (to ourselves and others) increases, and the amygdalae (clusters of grey matter in the brain that play a key role in emotion and behaviour) reduce in size and activation. We can observe these facts when we look at the brains of Buddhist monks who have meditated for thousands of hours. They tend to be much calmer when, for example, loud noises occur very near them. This proves that the benefits that happen during their practice continue in everyday life as well.

There is emerging evidence for ordinary people (as opposed to clinical populations) gaining statistically significant benefits from ten or more minutes of mindfulness practice a day. These ten minutes can lead to multiple improvements in efficiency, relationships and general wellbeing.

With practice, you will find that mindfulness offers an entirely new way to live; beyond soothing life's stresses, you may find it invites you to shift your whole way of thinking. You will begin to understand yourself more deeply, recognizing your thought-patterns, and will find that you relate to others in a more authentic way – with kindness and compassion.

Many people have tried to capture what mindfulness is. It could be defined as the basic human aptitude to be completely present, conscious of where one is and what one is doing, and in a mind-state that is neither overly reactive nor overcome by what is happening around us; it is observing "what is", right here and right now – free of judgement. In short, we could call it an experience of sustained awareness in the present moment, breath by breath!

Our modern definitions of mindfulness tend to over-focus on the aspect of attention and alertness, whereas the qualities of mindful awareness – such as acceptance, loving kindness and compassion (including self-compassion) – are important ingredients too, which should not be forgotten. I will include some compassion practices in this book, as this will offer a more balanced and truthful picture of what mindfulness is all about.

The clinical psychologist Chris Germer (who co-created the Mindful Self-Compassion training programme with educational psychologist Kristin Neff) trained me as a Mindful Self-Compassion teacher. He explained in one of his lectures that it is partially our language and the challenge of translation that may have contributed to a one-sided, almost sterile view of mindfulness. He clarified that "the word mindfulness is a translation of the ancient Pali word 'sati', which refers to awareness, and it is associated with (another) Pali word 'citta', which literally means 'heart–mind'." This latter word is absent from English and most other European languages, although we do use expressions such as "I feel something deeply in my heart" or "in my gut", which is in turn represented in phrases such as having a "heavy heart" or a "gut feeling". Germer and Neff's 2019 guide for professionals *Teaching the Mindful Self-Compassion Program* goes into more detail about the origin of the word "mindfulness".[2]

Most of us can vividly remember childhood memories when being mindful was natural – a given – whether we were totally absorbed in licking an ice cream or rolling down a grassy hill, experiencing every bump and this innate joy and laughter, the feeling of simply being alive. In those early years of childhood we were truly curious about life. But over time we generally lost this natural connection and it was replaced by expectations, tasks, even dreams, which as soon as they were achieved shed their fascination and tended to be replaced with new ones.

For most adults it is natural to experience life in "automatic pilot mode". We go about our business, are ruled by to-do lists and duties connected to our job or our relationships. Even when we think we are "free" and we engage in exercise or hobbies, often we are driven by goals that have to be achieved: how far we need to run, how much weight we need to lose, how to be at the top of the tennis-club table ... and the list goes on. By practising mindfulness, our intention is to reconnect with our ability to experience life as it unfolds, moment by moment. To *be* human, rather than a programmed action-machine.

You may find it rather odd to observe your breath, for example, because initially you are probably going to find out how active your brain is and how many thoughts – often negative ones (NATs = negative automatic thoughts, see page 100) – but also random memories or planning thoughts you have. In a word, there is a lot of mental chatter going on, while you are trying to focus on a "specific anchor of awareness", which might be your breath, sounds or walking.

I remember in detail how I got stuck while reciting a poem in a pre-school event – the sense of shame and anxiety I felt, and the heat that arose in my whole body and made my cheeks shine like rubies. I can still recall this event as if it occurred yesterday. Similarly I remember distinctly when I was accused of lying by a nun in my first year of primary school (aged around five) and the sense of desperation I felt in my whole body: trembling, a tight throat, flushed cheeks and the wish to shout at her (but not daring to) that she was wrong about me, that I was honest! It was the first time I understood that we cannot trust everybody who appears to be kind.

But once you can accept that these NATs have been there for many years, if not decades – that this is the nature of the "mental mind" (there is also a "heart" and "gut" mind) – you will find it possible to learn to work around them. Mindfulness is like waking up from autopilot, and if you remember learning to drive or learning an instrument or a language, you will begin to understand that it will take time to develop the "art of living in the present moment".

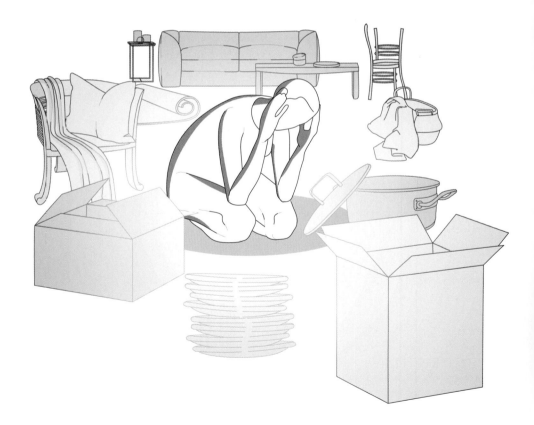

The Benefits of Mindfulness

There are so many ways in which mindfulness can benefit our lives. Here are some key benefits that will bring you a deep sense of self-empowerment:

1. Mindfulness strengthens different forms of attention (see page 14). There are three types of attention:
    - "Focused attention", when we use one of our senses as an anchor for our practice
    - "Sustained attention", when we keep returning again and again to the breath or the body (anchors), even though our thoughts have once again lured us away
    - "Selective attention" in more advanced practices, which will help us to focus first on one anchor and then switch to another

    For example, in the Body Scan (see page 196), we first use focused attention by starting with our feet, then sustained attention by feeling into them and seeing what we might find there: tingling, warmth, numbness and so on; and finally selective attention, when the mind has wandered off into planning or judging and we patiently escort it back to the foot or other parts of the body that we are focusing on.

2. We learn the art of "pausing", before immediately judging ourselves and others, when things don't go the way we might have hoped they would.

3. We start to observe our "thoughts", and perhaps at times manage to see that this "thinking" is not helpful, if it keeps feeding our anxiety or anger.

4. We also acquire the art of living in this moment, and thus become more deeply in touch with our life. Nowness and "presentness" become our new reality, at least for some of the time.

Many of us would probably agree that planning or list-making have their place, but can lead to us feeling out of control and rather stressed. Mindfulness helps us to focus on one thing at a time – each moment being a fresh experience. We are no longer ruled by failures of the past, or fear of the future, but receive the gift of now: the *present*.

Through mindfulness we can get to know ourselves and our patterns better, notice what we really "need" to know, let go of mindless chatter (at least some of the time), let our hearts be more open and moved by the suffering of others or ourselves, and be more prepared to lend a helping hand when and where it is needed. We will build up a strong core and will find it more natural to engage in helpful actions in all walks of life. We learn a deep awareness of the self, but simultaneously awareness of everything. We cannot control everything that happens to us, but we can change how we respond to it. We can choose to nurture kindness, peace and resilience, even during troubled times.

Thus mindfulness explores the cultivation of, and reconnection to, these basic human abilities through methods such as breath and body awareness, mindful movement, mindful eating and other activities (see the chapter Finding Joy and Mindful Activities on page 220). And, on a much larger scale, mindfulness may be an essential intervention that could help our whole species survive and sustain our planet.

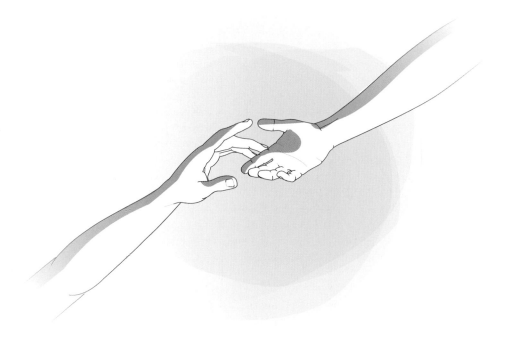

Pharmacist and mindfulness teacher Dr Karen Neil has kindly shared her insights with me, talking about social action and how we are all interconnected:

> The practice of mindfulness is extremely valuable during such challenging times, supporting people engaged in policy change to take care of themselves, become more aware of what depletes them and what is needed to maintain good health, prevent illness and burnout and, crucially, enabling them to make informed decisions. Without mindfulness, we are likely to fall victim to what Professor Paul Gilbert describes as "old brain functions", including anxiety and anger and "fight or flight" behaviour [see page 102], causing harm to ourselves and others.

> When we are stressed, we are less able to think clearly, dating back to the times when activation of the "fight or flight" system in the body was required to serve the "old brain function" of survival. Those were the days when our ancestors were often faced with life-and-death situations, encountering wild animals or rival tribes. It was not helpful to expend energy solving a complex problem, and our executive function therefore continues to be impaired when we feel threatened [see page 102].

> Mindfulness brings greater self-awareness and recognition of when we fall into old brain patterns of behaviour. It also provides a broadening of our understanding of who we are and how connected we are to others — our social brains impacted by each other with every interaction. Developing an awareness of our experience reveals more choice and the possibility of breaking out of automatic habit patterns that do not always serve us well. We can see more clearly what we are able to change, acting wisely from a place of knowing and intentionality, and moving toward more peaceful acceptance of what we are unable to influence. This is sometimes misunderstood as passivity, but is rather a more productive way of being, reducing the stress and suffering from anger or anxiety triggered by undesirable reality. It becomes possible to live life with greater balance or equanimity!

> It is problematic that, as Einstein observed, human beings experience a sense of separation, which he described as "a kind of optical delusion of his consciousness". This, he says, is "a kind of prison for us", and that "our task must be to free ourselves from this prison by widening our circles of compassion to embrace all living creatures and the whole of nature in its beauty".

> Mindfulness is often described as "wakefulness" and helps us to see reality more clearly, as discussed above. To begin to see for ourselves how interconnected we truly are to each other and, ultimately, the wider universe. When we look, it is possible to see the origins of ourselves and our world from stardust, and the absence of separation from the environment upon which we depend for life: from the oxygen in the air to the food from the Earth, the water cycle and life-giving warmth and light exuded by the sun.

Wise teachers are increasingly highlighting the potentially devastating consequences of continuing to see ourselves as "separate" and persisting with dualistic thinking of "us" and "them", from individual families to countries and continents. Again, when we look closely, we can see the impact of many of our actions on the wider world. Our love affair with travel and fossil fuels is now impacting the climate across the entire globe …

And yet, for many, there continues to be a narrow focus on material gain, wealth and competition, an economy into which we are educated to contribute. In 2020 there has been a wake-up call for humanity as to the fragility of modern society, with the rapid spread of Covid-19 …

Uncovering our ability to be aware reveals the power and benefits that flow from acting with integrity and compassion, as opposed to competitiveness or greed, leading to trust and respect and, ultimately, a safe space for open collaboration and learning from inevitable human mistakes.

With a clearer sight of reality, as though taking a panoramic view through a clean, wide-angled lens, wiser choices and decision-making become more likely. Acceptance of difference, welcoming religious, ethnic and neuro-diversity and our shared humanity, together with acting with kindness, fosters wise and collaborative action, taken intentionally for the benefit of not just greater wellbeing and flourishing, but ultimately our future survival on this planet.

Health given priority over wealth, longer-term decisions for the benefit of the wider world and precious planet, waking up to the fact that everything is connected and that ultimately our thoughts and actions impact on the whole world, these are vital steps forward. Einstein's observation referring to this delusion that leads to separation is so paramount! We breathe the same air, drink the same water and no matter how hard we try to shut out suffering in other parts of the world, we still feel it and are impacted by it at some deep level … We appear to be destroying ourselves with unsustainable population and economic growth. However, there is vast inherent intelligence and wisdom in many an untapped resource, waiting to be uncovered, with limitless potential for a bright future.

Mindfulness is a key to future prosperity and flourishing, by "waking us up" to a clear sight of reality and solutions, the inaccuracy of our unchallenged perceptions and the limitations of our primitive animal behaviours. Historical survival instincts have got us this far, but we need to step up, recognize their destructive impact and evolve into the best we can be, protecting our species and this special planet we are fortunate to call home.[3]

Love gives naught but itself and takes naught but from itself.
Love possesses not nor would it be possessed;
For love is sufficient unto love.
When you love you should not say, "God is in my heart,"
but rather, "I am in the heart of God."
And think not you can direct the course of love, for love,
if it finds you worthy, directs your course.
Love has no other desire but to fulfil itself.
But if you love and must needs have desires, let these be your desires:
To melt and be like a running brook that sings its melody to the night.
To know the pain of too much tenderness.
To be wounded by your own understanding of love;
And to bleed willingly and joyfully.
To wake at dawn with a winged heart and give thanks for another day of loving;
To rest at the noon hour and meditate love's ecstasy;
To return home at eventide with gratitude;
And then to sleep with a prayer for the beloved in your heart
and a song of praise upon your lips.

– Kahlil Gibran, Lebanese-American writer, poet,
visual artist and philosopher (1883–1931)[4]

Opening Up to a New Way of Living

The space between the idea of mindfulness and making changes to fit this practice into your life can be wide. You have bought this book and you want to experience the benefits of a new way of living, but that involves creating new habits. Often, when we aim to change our behaviour, our habits, we can meet resistance. Resistance can manifest as a fear of change, lack of determination, distractions, too many goals and disappointment at the lack of perceived progress. I like to view these forms of resistance as "hindrances".

Rather than seeing these "hindrances" as something negative perhaps view them as opportunities to grow? Facing resistance and acknowledging it is one of the first steps toward embracing mindfulness; working through resistance will make it easier to continue your journey of transformation and awareness. As your focus improves, and time passes, many manifestations of resistance will melt away.

When you experience your own particular type of "hindrances", you might like to note these down in your Mindfulness Journal. As you are beginning to learn, awareness is the first step to freedom and change.

Common Hindrances

In the following selection of "hindrances", I have given some suggestions for how to work through these challenges or, with your new way of thinking, opportunities for growth. Again, you may discover other approaches that appeal and are also effective for you.

Whatever your methods of moving forward toward change, enjoy learning to pause. When we stop to connect with ourselves in mindfulness, and find the stillness within, we can truly appreciate the power of being in the moment.

Fear of Change

Developing a mindfulness practice can be scary because it is making a commitment to change; it is acknowledging that how you are living your life now is not working. It is human nature to fear and resist change, it can feel more comfortable to stay with the familiar. The stress that comes from the idea of change is connected to uncertainty, the fear of the unknown and a lack of security. But it is the times when you feel the most fear that you are often on the verge of a break-through. Yes, an alarm bell is warning you that you are about to step outside of your comfort zone, but don't you want to keep exploring and discover what is on the other side?

When you feel fear, it can be helpful to remember that life ebbs and flows, change is constant and any feelings of fear will pass. The unfamiliar will soon become familiar, until you make new changes and then the cycle will begin all over again: instigating change, resistance, fear, moving forward and a familiarity of new behaviour/way of living.

Lack of Determination

Setting aside time to practise mindfulness requires determination. Initially, as you engage with your mindfulness practice you may find that your thoughts are scattered, and it can be tempting to give up. However, it can be helpful to remember that the brain is like a muscle and the more you use it in a certain way the stronger it will become. Learning step by step, it is only a matter of time until you will feel more fully connected in body, mind and spirit.

You may find it helpful to focus on being mindful during everyday tasks to boost your connection to this new way of being, and hopefully boost your ability to focus overall.

Distractions

You may feel it is a battle to create time for mindfulness due to distractions: problems in your life, challenging relationships, a noisy home or lack of privacy – the list is endless. All these distractions are the ideal opportunity for growth. Remember, you are on a journey and there are going to be distractions along the way, you may be led down a side-street but the main road is always there for you to find again. Use this book as your roadmap to mindfulness.

Too Many Goals

In your excitement, it can be tempting to set too many goals. Having goals is fantastic, but when you become attached to achieving particular outcomes it can distract you from your mindfulness practice. You may even start to feel frustrated, angry or negative. One way to combat these emotions is to focus on the good things – writing in your Gratitude Journal (see page 74) can re-anchor your emotions and help you feel a sense of satisfaction.

Disappointment and Lack of Progress

Should you feel a little disappointed at any moment of your journey, kindly remember that every moment is a new beginning! Please practise the Three-step Breathing Space (page 68) to reconnect yourself, and your thoughts, to the here and now. You can also read your Mindfulness Journal (see page 12) to look back on how far you have come on your journey.

Frequently Asked Questions

Here are some of the most-asked questions on practising mindfulness that you may find helpful as you begin your journey:

Question: "I don't have much time. How long do I need to practise mindfulness before I feel the benefits?"

Answer: True enough: mindfulness is not a quick fix. However, there are long-lasting benefits that you will experience by carving out 10, 20 or – eventually – 30 minutes a day by reducing other stress-creating activities such as watching a lot of television, reading the newspapers or engaging constantly with social-media activities.

Question: "I've been diagnosed with depression/other mental illness. What if mindfulness makes my symptoms worse?"

Answer: If you are vulnerable and suffer from anxiety, trauma, depression or other serious health conditions, books on the topic and apps that are available to download are only useful "add-ons" to studying with an *experienced mindfulness teacher*.

Question: "Do I need to understand Buddhism to practise mindfulness? I follow another religion and worry that mindfulness may not sit with my faith."

Answer: Many mindfulness meditations derive from Buddhist traditions, but you do not have to be Buddhist, or understand Buddhism, to practise secular mindfulness and enjoy the benefits it brings. There are both religious and philosophical types of Buddhism. Buddhism as a faith is about finding enlightenment and releasing the soul from the cycle of life, karma, death and rebirth. Without the religious connections, Buddhism as a philosophy is a path to personal development and encourages qualities like awareness, wisdom and kindness. Whatever the type of Buddhism, followers use similar practices, such as prayer, chanting, using and counting beads, that are present in all religions. And for all atheists who want to learn mindfulness, simply focusing on your breath or body sensations and observing your mind have nothing to do with believing in a higher power, but are, rather, human attributes.

Question: "I've never tried meditation before, will I be able to practise mindfulness properly?"

Answer: There is no right or wrong way to "do" mindfulness because it is a state of being, which manifests naturally with practice and repetition. Mistakenly, people often think of mindfulness as a meditation where you need to empty the mind. But mindfulness is not about emptying the mind (and rarely is meditation). Mindfulness is about being in the moment, developing an awareness of the body, enjoying the little things (and so much more) and, importantly, acknowledging your thoughts and sitting with them, or letting those thoughts drift away. As you work your way through this book, you will be drawn to certain exercises and discover the ones you enjoy most. Those exercises will become your "go-to" choices for your daily mindfulness practice. Kindly avoid dismissing an exercise because it feels harder – often facing difficulties can teach us the most important lessons about ourselves.

Question: "Can mindfulness help me to worry less?"

Answer: It is only human to worry sometimes. However, worrying can take up a lot of energy! In this mind-state you project your focus into the "future" and imagine what might happen. In fact, worrying is often described as "praying for what you don't want". Mindfulness assists you to remain in the present moment; it grounds you in the reality of what is happening, not what might happen. The practice of being mindful will help you stay calm and focused right here, right now.

Question: "Can mindfulness help me with my brain fog? Sometimes, I feel overwhelmed and find it hard to focus and make decisions."

Answer: Yes, most definitely! Brain fog, an inability to think clearly, forgetfulness and so on, is a type of mental fatigue, which is often triggered by stress. Mindfulness aims to reduce stress and brings your focus to the "here and now". The guided meditations in this book will help you to rediscover your mental clarity and find the stillness within that is present in all of us no matter how hectic our lives may seem.

To see a world in a grain of sand,
And a heaven in a wild flower,
Hold infinity in the palm of your hand
And eternity in an hour.

– William Blake, English painter, poet and visionary (1757–1827)[1]

A Mindful Day

This chapter is your main resource centre, particularly if you are new to mindfulness. Do read and use it as often as possible, and gradually start to implement any steps that are possible for you.

By bringing mindfulness into your daily activities, you will have a much richer – and often calmer – experience of life. Let this chapter be an invitation to you to try something out. *Even if you only manage one activity per day initially*, and then over a period of weeks and months you expand it to longer periods, you will probably feel a deeper sense of being alive and connected to all things. And don't forget to keep your Mindfulness Journal (see page 12) to hand, and to use it on a regular basis. I know, from experience, that the more you engage in your practice, the better it gets.

When I began my yoga and meditation journey I was driven by a wish to be the best mum I could be for my son, who had recently been diagnosed with autism. I also wanted to be the most loving mother for my other son and make sure that I devoted special time to him, too. Lastly, I figured that I needed to have some chill time solely for myself. I allotted specific periods in my diary for just ten minutes of yoga, Body Scan or breath practice a day. Often I noticed that I had unknowingly practised for longer – 12, 15 or even 20 minutes. So be mindful of the fact that you can lose the notion of "time" when you are practising being truly in the moment. If you have another important appointment booked, use an alarm clock to remind you to stop your mindfulness practice. You'll see: it *is* possible to be prepared!

This chapter includes lots of advice about how to start your day mindfully, as well as advice to help get you through the day. In the evening, take plenty of time to slow down and unplug yourself from technology. There is a whole chapter later in the book on mindful sleep (see page 164). Please make use of it.

A Mindful Morning

The first thing you do when you wake up will set the tone for your day. Are you going to select the calm option or the stressed default? With this concept in mind, it can be a good habit to start your morning mindfully. You may want to run through a mental list of three things you are grateful for before you even get out of bed; you may wish to take a few deep breaths to connect with your body awareness or set a mindful intention for the day. Here's my own concept of the ideal mindful morning.

Upon waking (hopefully without a shrill alarm), bring your awareness to your breathing. Stay in a comfortable posture and allow each breath to unfold, moment by moment. Do this before you're tempted to check your phone, and before you become overwhelmed with digital information. Give yourself this space to really breathe and reconnect with yourself after sleep.

The Benefits of Breathing Practice

One very good way to reduce your susceptibility to stress is through your breathing: 70 per cent of all debris that our body produces, which could potentially harm it, can be expelled through the breath. Only 20 per cent of all waste products leave the body through the skin, and just 10 per cent through the digestive system – a fascinating insight.

Another important fact is that, normally, human beings breathe between 12 and 16 times per minute. If, however, someone is very stressed, they may breathe up to 100 times per minute. This is called "hyperventilation", and in the worst-case scenario it can lead to a panic attack or fainting.

If we breathe nice and calmly, we breathe in about 1 litre (1¾ pint) of air on one long in-breath. Every time we breathe in deeply and slowly, our diaphragm expands and starts massaging organs such as the liver, kidneys and stomach. And every time we breathe in through our nostrils (our nasal passages have loads of tiny little hairs that act as a filter), we cleanse the air of dust particles and there is less danger of bacteria entering our throat and lungs. Most Eastern breathing techniques therefore recommend breathing in and out through your nostrils – as with yoga breathing and Tai Chi. Should you find this difficult, close your mouth and make a slim opening between your lips, so that you can breathe in and out gently. Imagine blowing on a spoonful of hot soup. Be very gentle!

Many philosophies and modern teachers of exercise tell you to take a deep breath and relax … This common wisdom is based on a principle called the Hering–Breuar Reflex. When you inhale fully and slowly, stretch receptors in your lungs signal relaxation in your cardiovascular system. They also trigger a decrease in your heart rate and lower your blood pressure. In addition, deep breathing floods your body with oxygen, which is, after all, its primary fuel. It opens your chest and allows a more relaxed form of breathing. Simple breathing alone can calm your mind and nourish your body at any time. By repeatedly stimulating the vagus nerve – the nerve that extends from the brainstem to the abdomen – during those long exhalations, slow breathing can shift the nervous system toward a more restful, stress-free state.

Practice: Mindful Breathing

Mindful, steady breathing is a powerful way to reduce stress and lower blood pressure, bringing feelings of calm and wellbeing. This practice can transport you into the present moment; rather than revisiting last night's dream or starting to plan the day ahead, you can simply "be".

Duration: 5–10 minutes

1. Choose a place in your home where you feel peaceful and undisturbed. You may stay in your bed or sit on a chair, or lie down on the floor; leaning against a wall to support your spine is wonderful, too. Make sure you keep warm, so perhaps wrap a shawl or blanket around you. You may wish to light a candle. Finding stillness by bringing awareness to your breath is the focus of this exercise.

2. Try and sit (unless you have chosen an alternative posture) in a comfortable upright position, feeling a sense of dignity and letting your shoulders drop. Gently close your eyes, if this feels comfortable, or keep them in soft focus, as an alternative.

3. Now bring your awareness to feeling your body as a whole, focusing your attention on the sensations of touch where your body makes contact with the floor or whatever you are sitting/lying on. Spend a few minutes exploring these sensations. Simply feel into your body and let it breathe.

4. Gently move to your head and face. First sense the top of your head and the hair follicles, the back of your head, then your forehead, and have the intention to smooth it out with gentle imaginary strokes. You may like to imagine chocolate lying on the windowsill and the rays of the sun melting it slowly, just like that smoothing – soothing your forehead. Now move your awareness to your eyes, softening your eyebrows, eyeballs, eyelids ... Continue this process by smoothing out your cheeks and your jaw; letting all tension go, allowing your whole face to become loose. Bring awareness to your mouth, with the gums and tongue relaxed, the teeth and finally your lips, soft and loose ... Soften all your facial muscles as best as you can. Now briefly send this sense of softness to your neck and throat, the chest and abdomen, the shoulders, arms and hands, and then to your legs, feet and toes. In this softened state of awareness, I am now inviting you to start focusing on your breathing.

5. Notice the soft in-breath and, as you inhale, the chest and even the abdomen rising; and then, on the out-breath, the same areas falling down, emptying ... Keep your attention on your breathing, "being with" each in-breath for its full duration and with each out-breath for its full duration, as if you are riding the waves of your own breathing. Keep doing this for five rounds (one in- and one out-breath makes one round).

6. What happens if your mind wanders off into thinking, daydreaming or planning? At those moments you have briefly lost touch with your breathing, but that is okay and is quite normal. Calmly notice what it was that took you away from focusing on your breathing; then gently and kindly, and without judgement, return your focus to your breathing once again. Here is another moment to begin anew!

7. Having tried all this, you may wish to start noticing the gentle change in temperature around the tip of your nose, at your nostrils; on the inflow, the air will probably feel cooler than on the outflow. Continue this for five rounds.

8. Whenever you notice the wandering mind, return to your anchor of attention: the breath. It is just as valuable to become aware that your mind has wandered, and bring it back to the breath, as it is to remain aware of the breath. After all, only someone who is being mindful will ever notice the wandering nature of the mind. This reminds me of trying to gently rein in a wild horse, and training it to bear a saddle and not run off and hurt itself. The training is gentle, kind and ongoing. Who would ever want to break this beautiful wild horse? Kindly taming it, without breaking its spirit, is the aspiration.

9. Now bring your attention to the beginning and end of each breath: there will be a little pause after each in-breath and another little pause after each out-breath. Focus on this for about five rounds. Do not try to expand or deepen your breathing artificially during this practice. Simply allow it to unfold naturally. So some breaths will be shorter and shallower, others longer and deeper. Each breath has "a life of its own" and thus differs from any other breath. It is a total moment-to-moment experience when you sit with your breathing.

10. If possible, continue for a little while longer if you have the time, enjoying the surf of your breathing coming and going, then finally bringing this practice to an end. Once again get in touch with your whole body, its position and the points of contact with the surface you are resting on.

11. Now gently stretch a little, with calm awareness. Open your eyes and start the new day without rushing. When you are ready, sit up carefully and place your feet mindfully on the floor. Upon standing, you may feel like stretching a little more.

Now proceed with this moment-to-moment alertness throughout your day. Obviously each person has their own routine; please adapt your daily routine however feels appropriate for you.

Mindful Morning Routine

You can turn your everyday morning routine into a mindfulness practice. Become aware of the small things that you do after you wake up, and really bring your attention to them; you'll begin to see and appreciate your surroundings with fresh eyes. The suggestions below are great if you're new to mindfulness, helping you to slow down small actions with which you are already familiar.

- Walking over and opening the curtains and the window can be seen as a daily new adventure. Bring curiosity and non-judgement to whatever weather conditions await you. If it is mild or sunny, smile and breathe in the rays of the sun and the fresh air. If it is raining or snowing, remember that all beings and the soil need water. So breathe in the damp, cool air with gratitude.

- You may now want to prepare the clothes you wish to wear today. Perhaps you choose some of your favourite items and arrange them on your bed, before proceeding to go to the bathroom. Notice each step: lifting, shifting and placing the sole of each foot, moment by moment. Isn't it marvellous that the body knows exactly how to do this "walking" (see Mindful Walking on page 108)?

- Are you going to have a shower or a bath? Whatever you decide, bring mindfulness to the temperature of the water, how it gently revives your skin and cleans it. Are you using a special soap or fragrant oil? Bring awareness to the smell – is it refreshing, soothing, both, or simply pleasant? Try as best you can to be fully present when you have this experience. Avoid making lists for the rest of the day, or jumping ahead with thoughts connected to whatever action will follow next. This moment in the bathroom really matters – it is now that you are truly alive!

- Bring special tender attention to drying your whole body – as if you are doing a mini Body Scan (see page 196).

- Brush your teeth with loving awareness: tasting the toothpaste or tooth oil, feeling the rotation of the toothbrush and attending to each tooth for a little while.

- If you need to shave, kindly bring gentle attention to this action, too.

- Enjoy putting on your face cream/aftershave – all of this is a precious gift to comfort your being.

- Get dressed mindfully, with each item slowly covering your body, protecting it and keeping it warm (or cool). Relish this process – not only because you have these wonderful garments, but also because you are able to take delightful care of yourself.
- Now complete your waking-up process with some gentle movement. If you have a regular movement practice, you already know what to do: stretching, Chi Gong, Tai Chi, yoga or Pilates, for instance.

On the following page is a humble movement practice that I love doing early in the day, called "Simple Sun Salutation".

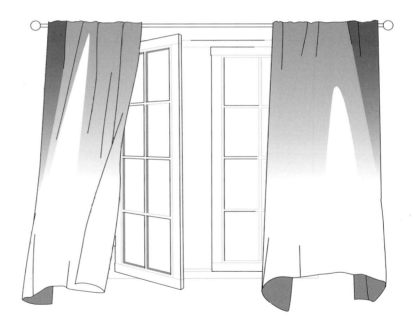

Practice: Simple Sun Salutation

This is my mindfulness version of the classic yoga sequence, traditionally practised at sunrise to awaken mind, body and spirit to the day ahead. The gentle stretches help you come into your body: a perfect way to feel at one with yourself and the world around you. Please only engage in this practice if your body feels well and flexible. If not, you can always sit down and internally visualize the physical practices, as if you were doing them. Even this will regulate your nervous system and help your flow of endorphins (wellbeing chemicals). If possible, practise this exercise on a yoga mat or carpet. Find your own way to do this movement, paying attention to how you feel and what your body needs at each stage.

Duration: 12–15 minutes

1. Stand upright, with soft shoulders, a soft face, your hands in the Prayer Position and your feet hip-width apart.

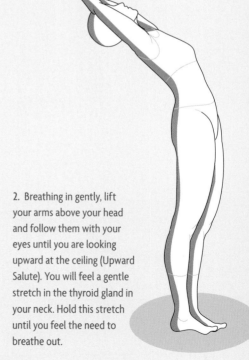

2. Breathing in gently, lift your arms above your head and follow them with your eyes until you are looking upward at the ceiling (Upward Salute). You will feel a gentle stretch in the thyroid gland in your neck. Hold this stretch until you feel the need to breathe out.

3. Breathe in once more and then, on the out-breath, slowly bend forward, rolling your spine down, vertebra by vertebra, bending your knees as much as you need to, until your fingertips reach the ground (Forward Fold). Breathe in and out.

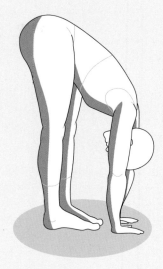

4. On the next in-breath, stretch further down, placing your hands with stretched fingers to the left and right of your left knee and, on the out-breath, moving your right leg and foot toward the back, stretching them as far back as is comfortable for you (Lunge). Never enter a painful zone. Breathe in.

5. During the next out-breath, let your left leg follow your right, so that both are stretched backward (Plank Position). An easier option is to come down onto your knees, which will serve as a second support to your feet and put less pressure on your wrists. Always listen carefully to your body and stop striving!

6. Breathe in and, on the next out-breath, gently slide down completely onto the floor, lying on your belly, with the forehead down and the feet relaxed (Staff Pose). Rest for a few in- and out-breaths.

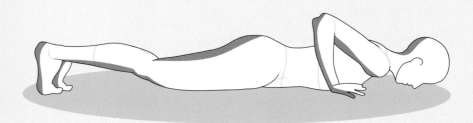

7. On the next in-breath, place your hands firmly to the left and right of your chest and push into the floor, bending and very gently tilting your head and neck upward (gentle Cobra Pose). Rest in this posture for a few breaths.

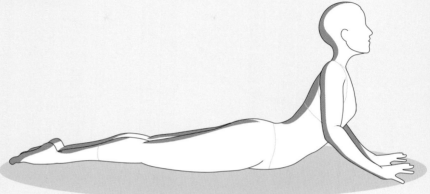

8. On the next out-breath come up into a kneeling box position. Then breathe in gently and push your buttocks upward. This should feel comfortable for you at this moment, so bent knees are absolutely fine (Down Dog Pose). Breathe in and out a couple of times.

9. On an out-breath, gently push the right leg forward and place the foot on the ground between your hands, as far as it will go without forcing it (Lunge).

10. Breathe in and let your other leg follow, so that both legs are now between your dangling head and arms (Forward Fold).

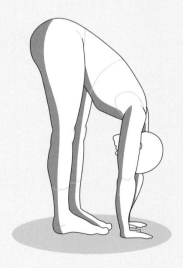

11. Breathe in and out and, while doing this, very slowly roll your spine and head upward until you are standing upright again.

12. To complete a whole round, do the same routine again, only reversed, with your left leg going back first. Each half-round combines 11 yoga positions smoothly, making 22 poses in a full round. I really recommend doing this practice as slowly and mindfully as possible. Eventually, over a period of a week or longer, you can build up your stamina to a maximum of five rounds.

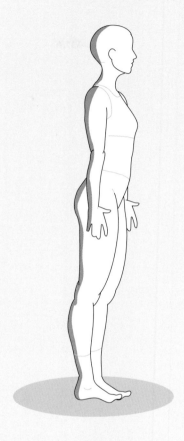

This stretching and cardiovascular practice will release a lot of the hormone adrenaline and a great deal of tension. When you stand in your final upright pose (often referred to as the Mountain Pose), there is a great possibility that you will be feeling and thinking much more calmly, yet you will be alert and will maybe even feel as strong and peaceful as a mountain.

Once you are familiar with the individual steps in the Simple Sun Salutation (see pages 54–59), you can use this visual reminder for the complete sequence.

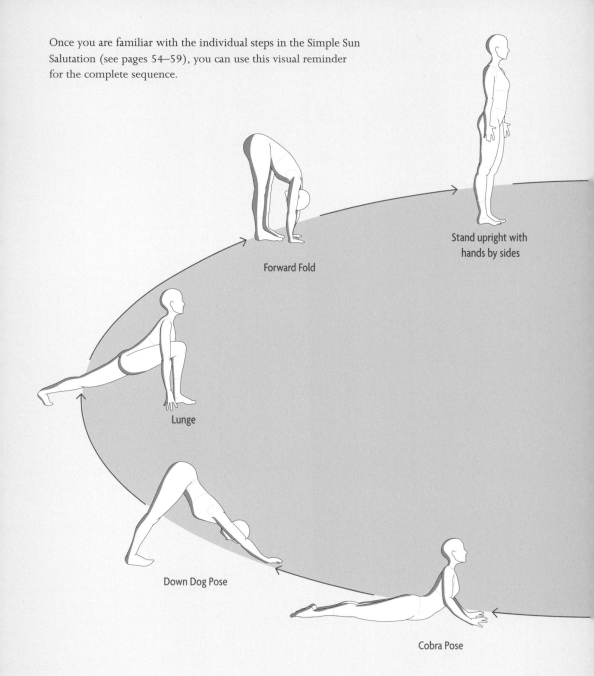

Forward Fold

Stand upright with hands by sides

Lunge

Down Dog Pose

Cobra Pose

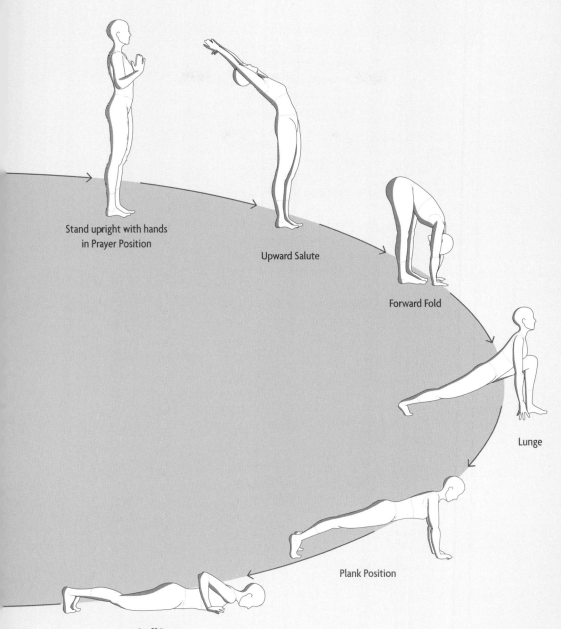

Stand upright with hands in Prayer Position

Upward Salute

Forward Fold

Lunge

Plank Position

Staff Pose

I'll tell you how the sun rose, –
A ribbon at a time.
The steeples swam in amethyst,
The news, like squirrels, ran.

The hills untied their bonnets,
The bobolinks begun.
Then I said softly to myself,
"That must have been the sun!"

But how he set, I know not.
There seemed a purple stile
Which little yellow boys and girls
Were climbing all the while

Till when they reached the other side,
A dominie in gray
Put gently up the evening bars,
And led the flock away.

– Emily Dickinson, American poet (1830–1886)[1]

Practice: Raisin Exercise

Before you decide what to eat or drink for breakfast, please engage in the following meditative eating practice. This way of engaging with a regular routine, such as eating, will open your eyes to how much more we deeply experience an action if we slow it down and savour it. To practise this exercise, you will need two or three raisins.

Duration: 5 minutes

1. Look at the raisins with childlike curiosity. What are you aware of when doing this? Do any emotions, thoughts or body sensations arise?

2. Now really focus on a couple of the raisins: perhaps pick them up and feel their weight and texture. Do they look the same, in size, shape or colour? Can you squeeze one, pull it apart, feel the ridges on the surface?

3. Feeling its surface structure between your thumb and forefinger, what are you noticing? Smoothness or roughness – or something sticky perhaps?

4. Touch your lips with a raisin. How does the sensation on the surface of your lips vary from the surface sensation on your finger? Is it different? Are your lips more sensitive than the surface of your fingers? Both areas are covered with skin, but nevertheless you may notice that your sensory perception varies.

5. Guide the raisin closer to your nostrils, exploring its smell. Is there a particular aroma that you become aware of? Is it pleasant or not? Maybe there is no smell at all?

6. Gently guide the raisin close to your ear, and start squeezing or rubbing it? Do you notice the little sound that sometimes arises? If you do, what emotion does it trigger in you? Are you giggling?

7. Move the raisin close to your mouth and notice how your body becomes alert and knows exactly when to open the mouth. See what your tongue does to receive the raisin, and how it finally rests peacefully on your tongue. Are you already noticing a taste before you start biting into the raisin? Do you notice saliva building up?

8. Take a first bite. Does the flavour explode in your mouth? What zests do you notice? Do you love it, dislike it or are you indifferent to it? Any response is fine; simply notice it with curiosity.

9. Continue chewing this one raisin until it has become a pulpy, soft texture, then slowly get ready to instruct your body to swallow it. Again observe how the body does this. Do you notice the raisin landing in your tummy? Do you feel you are satisfied now, or do you wish to eat another raisin? What thoughts, body sensations and feelings are you aware of? Has your breathing slowed down? Are you feeling playful and childlike?

10. When you have written down a few observations in your journal, it is time to transfer this way of eating mindfully to having your breakfast. Enjoy!

Moving on with Your Day

As I am a psychotherapist and mindfulness teacher I often work from home. So after breakfast I usually start doing some office work. I may answer emails or text messages and then make some phone calls (talking to new clients or arranging appointments). It is very important to engage in work activities with an attitude of openness, curiosity and kindness toward ourselves and the person we are intending to speak or write to. I invite you to take a few mindful in- and out-breaths before you dial the number or put fingers to keyboard. Try to be present, without fixed expectations. You do not know what mood the other person is going to be in.

By having started your day with an attitude of awareness and kindness, you will be able to stay calm, even if the other person happens to be stressed or short during your conversation. You will not, as it were, "take the bait" in that moment, and will pause before you respond. Your ability to understand the other person's predicament, and show patience and acceptance, may even change the energy of the whole conversation and be therapeutic and healing. Always intend to speak from the heart. I lived in China for a long time, and if you translate the Chinese word for mindfulness into English, it actually means "being present with the heart".

Continue your morning until lunchtime with awareness. Take breaks every 45 minutes or so and feel free to practise the Three-step Breathing Space (see page 68) whenever you need a break or to clear your head. For the rest of the day you may want to use some of the other tools laid out throughout the book. To incline the mind on joyful moments, please fill in a Pleasant-event Diary (see page 120) once or twice a day. For learning how to revolutionize your relationship with food, please browse through pages 150–162.

Kindly make some time in your day for exercise, pastimes, connecting with nature and meeting friends, whenever possible in the afternoon. For this you will find useful tips in the chapter Finding Joy and Mindful Activities (see page 220). And finally, almost everything you might want to know about sleep can be found in the chapter Mindfulness for Connecting with Sleep (see page 164).

I wish you a truly mindful day!

Practice: Three-step Breathing Space (1)

This short practice can be done while sitting, standing or walking – it can quickly restore calm when you feel stressed or overwhelmed. You can also use this technique if you need energy or some mental clarity to solve a problem.

Before you begin, draw an image of an hourglass in your journal and label it as follows:

- Mark the top section of the hourglass (the wide part) with a letter "A" for Awareness
- Mark the middle section of the hourglass (the narrow part) with a letter "G" for Gathering
- Mark the bottom section of the hourglass (the wide part) with a letter "E" for Expanding

Have you noticed the acronym AGE above? It will help you to remember the Three-step Breathing Space. Do this exercise three times a day.

Duration: 3–5 minutes

1. **Awareness:** Ask yourself: what am I thinking, feeling or sensing in my body right now?

2. **Gathering**: Now engage in Mindful Breathing (see page 50). The breath is your anchor. Practise at least five rounds of mindful in- and out-breathing to settle yourself and feel more at ease.

3. **Expanding:** Get a sense of your body and the space it takes up as a whole, as if you were using a pencil and were drawing a line around the outer edges of your body. Say to yourself, "This is my space. This is me and I am strong." Feel your feet deeply grounded, almost as if roots are growing out of the soles of your feet and into the floor. Now visualize an image of strength: a tree, a mountain or the calm sea.

Practise this exercise regularly, so that if the going gets rough and your brain shuts down, due to stress chemicals that are being released, you will know it by heart and can apply it, wherever you find yourself: in a traffic jam, an overcrowded bus, in a long queue in the supermarket, before an exam, a new date or an interview. This mini-meditation does not require you to sit upright and dignified; simply do it whenever you need to reset the stress button and find calm.

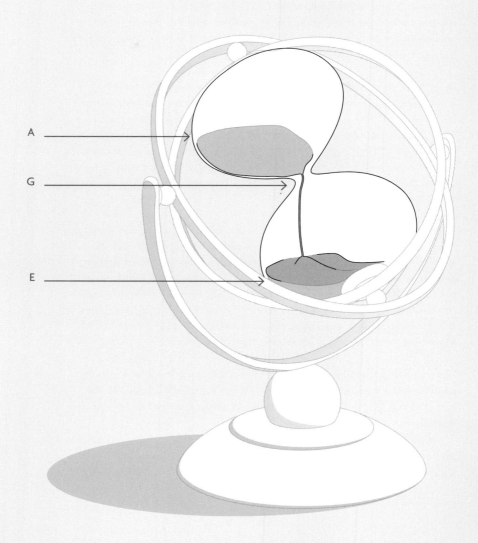

Breaking Habits with Mindfulness

Another wonderful outcome of becoming more mindful is breaking unwanted habits. Initially habits are so automatic that you may not even notice they are there, and often they get in the way of our ease and peace. None of us were born with habits; our brain slowly develops them over time. First something triggers a behaviour to unfold and it occurs. Then there is a reward, otherwise you would not continue engaging in this behaviour. Over time a neuropathway has developed.

Being more deeply conscious of your feelings and desires gives you a better starting point if you wish to begin breaking unhelpful habits. Use your journal (see page 12) and write down which bad habits immediately come to mind: for example, smoking, comfort eating, procrastinating, having negative thoughts about yourself (see NATs on page 100), always blaming others or yourself. Alas, there are some subtle behaviours of which you will need to become deeply mindful before you are able to "catch them", but the practices described here can help you begin to do this.

Once you have established at least a few unwanted habits that you wish to address, it can be really helpful to comprehend what initially triggered them. Not all are simply unhealthy habits for body or mind; some habits steal from us: time, attention and even relationships. Mindfully ask yourself what these patterns serve? Are you avoiding something, so that you cannot fail? Are you envious of what others have, or can do? Have you perhaps copied a trait that an early caregiver used to have? By becoming more aware, you might notice that stress is often not only a trigger, but also a "reinforcer" of those unwanted behaviours.

Use your journal to write down your intentions and goals. Try to be realistic. If a bad habit has been with you for decades, it won't magically go away. We are mammals and thus we respond well to rewards, compassion and positive self-talk. You will best deal with bad habits in three steps:
1. *Acknowledge* them
2. Notice *when* they happen most frequently
3. Then *replace* them with something more beneficial to you and other people

Do not be despondent if this does not always work immediately. Even acknowledging bad habits is a step in the right direction. As you will read later in the book, our brain can be rewired, and we have numerous studies that prove this. Your neural pathways developed over years and now respond to certain triggers. With mindfulness you can create new pathways, and the old ones might "overgrow", like old paths in the jungle that nobody uses any longer.

This will probably take some time, but you can simply address one habit at a time. On average it takes more than two months of regular practice before a new behaviour becomes automatic, but this will be so worthwhile for you. Take control of a habit that's been running you and you will be rewarded with a wonderful sense of self-empowerment. And remember that you have the rest of your life to engage with mindfulness.

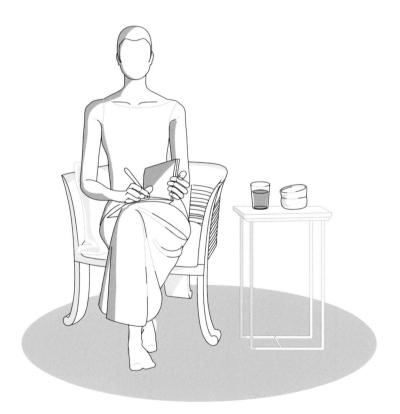

How Can Mindfulness Change My Experience of Being Alive?

Would you like to find out what makes you tick, and what makes you happy or drains you? Give yourself time to discover which meditations and everyday mindfulness practices really work for you. Reconnecting to some hobbies and pastimes that you used to love, or always wanted to try, can be really wonderful (see the chapter Finding Joy and Mindful Activities on page 220). Intentionally increasing those resources will lead to a calmer way of living step-by-step. And consider the following statements:

- I want to feel less tension in my body and know that I will "clear out the cupboard of past regrets".
- I would like to feel less dependent on others' appraisal of me and become more self-reliant.
- I want to become a better listener, a better friend, a kinder human being overall – somebody people seek to be with.
- I wish to cope better when the going gets rough.
- I would like to become more compassionate not only toward others, but also toward myself. How can I treat myself to special experiences, simply because I am worth it? What would it take for me to feel really content?

Be creative and see what little moments of mindfulness you can start building into your day: while working, shopping, travelling, taking breaks and at any time when you eat (lunch, dinner, snacks, tea and coffee breaks).

Finally, explore points of refuge (see page 14) that you can access: friends, family, retreats, Sangha (having other people to meditate with, both actually and online), Finding Joy and Mindful Activities (see page 220) or savouring the simple breath of life at certain moments throughout the day.

Finding the Time

In case you wonder where you will "find" the time to do all this, I have some mildly upsetting news for you: time cannot be found, but you can create it. Write down in your journal which aspects of your daily routine could be reduced in order to make space for meditating and slowing down: morning, noon, afternoon, evening. We are all different, and we will therefore choose different moments throughout the day. Could you possibly spend less time on social media, emails, watching TV, listening to the news or reading the newspapers? Just a little less, so that you free up some time for meditation and being more mindful.

As you have seen, practices such as the Three-step Breathing Space (see page 68) take only a few moments. And mindfulness will help you with time challenges: with practice, your mind will wander less and you will begin to manage your time more efficiently. You will find that you waste less time procrastinating and begin to use time more effectively, making the time that you need for yourself.

Developing a Gratitude Practice

One practice to add at any point in a mindful day is to spend time pondering gratitude – for all that life regularly offers you. Even challenges can often lead to deep insights.

Being grateful daily and counting your blessings, taking a moment to be present, can help you to feel less overwhelmed by life. Developing a "gratitude attitude" can create a sense of being more open and curious too, allowing you to celebrate the present rather than living in the past or the future. It will also help you embrace your life now, in the moment, which in turn can help positive energy to flow because gratitude blocks toxic, and draining, negative emotions.

One easy way to develop a gratitude practice is to keep a Gratitude Journal. Start simply – once a week list five things that you are grateful for and build from here to a daily entry. Some people write a daily gratitude letter, as if writing to a friend, while others prefer to stick with a straightforward list.

There are many other ways you can develop a gratitude practice. I have always liked the author Mary Jane Ryan's "Top Ten Ways to Become More Grateful".[2] The following suggestions for how to develop a gratitude practice are adapted from the things I learned while participating in one of her workshops.

- Focus on what feels good in your life, instead of what feels difficult.
- Take a moment to say one thing that you are thankful for at every mealtime.
- Say "thank you" to others as often as possible throughout the day.
- When a special person in your life – your spouse, kids or friends – is frustrating you, remember why you love them.
- Avoid comparing yourself, or your life, to others. When envy arises, ask yourself: how can I create more in me of what I see in them?
- Give thanks for your body. What can you appreciate about it right now?
- When difficult things happen, ask yourself: what can I learn from this? Even if it is very challenging, is there any silver lining in sight? If not, can I accept that this too will pass?
- Remember a situation in your life that was difficult to live through. How did it help you grow?

- Imagine how would you spend and treasure this day, if it was the last day of your life.
- Practise writing a kind note, card or letter daily to somebody who may really need or appreciate it. When we directly share our appreciation with others, it becomes even stronger. This is because transforming a thought into words or actions deepens its impact. The other person gets the benefit of your communication, and you not only deepen gratitude, but also the connection between you.

Look well to this one day,
For it, and it alone, is life.
In the brief course of this one day
Lie all the verities,
All the realities of your existence –
The joy of living,
The splendour of beauty,
The glory of action.
Yesterday is but a dream.
Tomorrow is but a vision.
But today, well-lived,
Will make every yesterday
A dream of happiness and
Each tomorrow a vision of hope.
Look well, therefore,
To this one day,
For it and it alone,
Is Life!

– Unknown

2

RELATIONSHIPS AND MENTAL WELLBEING

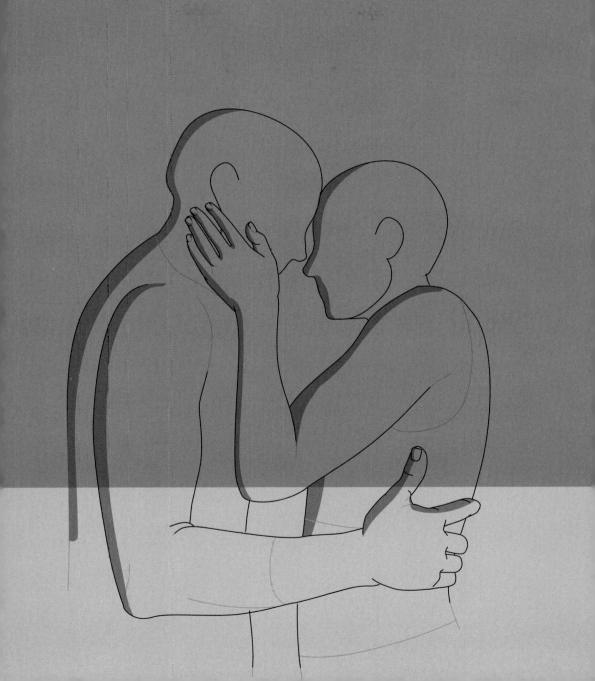

Mindfulness for Secure Relationships

Linking an attitude of mindful awareness to how we act and communicate with others has been shown to improve relationships overall. A 2004 University of North Carolina study of "relatively happy, non-distressed couples" showed that couples who practised mindfulness saw improvements to their "relationship happiness and coping with stress, feeling overall more harmonious".[1]

As mentioned previously, mindfulness increases our awareness of all our experiences and allows us a breathing space to decide how we want to respond in certain situations. Envisage, perhaps, being "triggered" to react to something by your partner. You may find yourself feeling that it is all too much, and doubting the worth of the relationship overall. You may feel despondent, angry, anxious, lost. As this is a full-blown stress response, the brain is unable to access the prefrontal cortex, which moderates social behaviour, and compassion and self-compassion will seem distant concepts.

Now imagine applying the Three-step Breathing Space (see page 68). This is exactly why I recommend practising it several times a day, so that you can use it in moments of distress. Suddenly you will notice your breathing slowing down; you may feel as if you are stepping out of a mist and you will be more aware of your emotions. You may even find it possible to refrain from reacting in the moment. Slowly you will be able to decide quite calmly how you would like to respond. You are no longer a victim of inept, forceful or even aggressive reactions and will find yourself dealing with this particular situation, rather than going down the "bad memory lane" where all past hurts and upsets are recalled as in a horror movie.

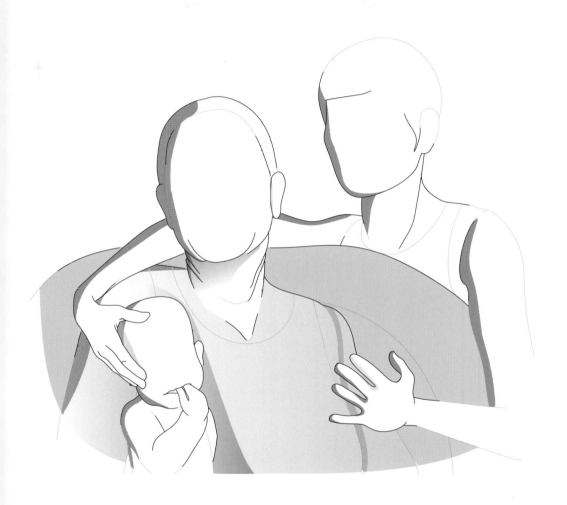

Because we generally feel "secure" with our partner, we may at times find ourselves being less than diplomatic during arguments and may say – or even do – things for which we later feel sorry. It seems that our most intimate relationships can present us with major challenges in our interactions with others.

Mindfulness is a wonderful tool for addressing the regular challenge of living with others. By becoming more focused and calmer, and by taking a pause, we can learn peaceful communication and can really see the situation from both sides. We may even decide together to let something be for now, until we have both settled down, and then agree on a date for resolving the problem to the best of our ability. As we have seen, the Three-step Breathing Space is a fast intervention that you can call upon when a problem arises suddenly; whereas a mindful walk (see page 108) will take you physically away from the situation, perhaps offering a new perspective on it.

After having had time to reflect, deeply noticing what you are really feeling, you may even be able to sit and write down your thoughts, either in your journal or in a letter to the other person. You never actually need to send this letter, but writing it often helps you gain a bigger perspective and better insights into an unresolved issue. You may even be able to see recurring patterns and then, at a pre-arranged meeting, decide a new way forward together. Mindfulness teaches us again and again that nothing lasts forever, and that every moment is a fresh beginning.

Mindfulness expert Dr Donna Rockwell has shared the value of mindfulness in the way it affects relationships. In an interview for PsychAlive.org she said, "What mindfulness does is it creates this space, it takes us out of the catastrophe … There's a lot more heart available. There's a lot more understanding possible than this need to defend."[2] We can nurture understanding, awareness and ethics within ourselves and extend these compassionate attitudes to those we love. With repeated practice of mindfulness meditation we can achieve a greater sense of inner peace that will benefit all beings around us.

Mindfulness and Intimacy

Thomas Bien, a wonderful mindful therapist, writes in his book *Mindful Recovery: A Spiritual Path to Healing from Addiction*: "Society is as neurotic about sex as it ever was."[3] As in so many other areas of our life, sex can become overtly goal-orientated: unless both partners climax, it does not count. When you watch a film where intimacy occurs, it is quite amazing how quickly, and perfectly, most scenes portray sex.

From a mindful perspective, we want to encourage people to experiment with "sensate focus", a technique that works by refocusing people on their own sensuality rather than on achieving goals. You are invited to engage mainly in touching and being touched, and in allowing yourself to enjoy this for at least half an hour. You focus on breathing mindfully, stroking and massaging your partner with deep awareness, and concentrate on the whole body rather than solely on the sexual areas. Of course these are not suddenly cut off, but they are only one part of the whole. You should close your eyes when receiving this and really sense the pleasure that is being offered to you, then reverse the process after a while. After this body-communication, it would be lovely if you could share with one another how you felt on both giving and receiving touch. Journaling would also be helpful.

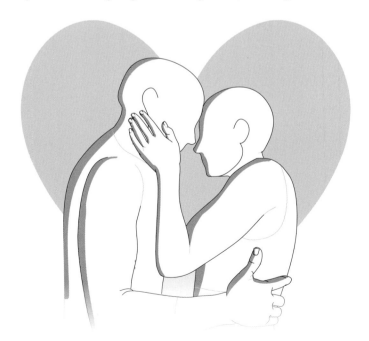

One

only one day
only one hour
only one moment
one song or poem
one smile, one kiss
being touched
with an ice cube
smelling rose tea
a spoon of ice cream
dunking biscuits in coffee
noticing your smile
and your eyes
tenderness
one and one
one

– Patrizia Collard

Mindfulness and Parenting

I cannot think about this topic without recalling the famous words of the Lebanese-American writer, poet, visual artist and philosopher Kahlil Gibran in his book of prose-poetry fables *The Prophet*: "Your children are not your children. They are the sons and daughters of Life's longing for itself ... You are the bows from which your children as living arrows are sent forth."[4] He makes it quite clear that our responsibility lies in looking after the arrows, sending them forth but accepting – just as we do with suffering or other challenges – that we cannot decide where the wind, or their purpose, will carry them.

In this insight lies some freedom. Yes, we are responsible for our offspring and, particularly in the early years, children need a lot of support and protection. But in the end they have their own journey, their own challenges to handle and their own desires that will guide them.

As mindful parents, we need to listen deeply when we have newborns or toddlers. They will be able to give us pre-verbal clues, but we need to try and respond to them with patience – not only because most of us have not been taught "the art of parenting", but also because we may not "get it": we may not comprehend what their crying or distress is all about. Sometimes we simply need to be there and hold them, and the comfort of this compassionate act may be enough for them.

Mindfulness is expressed in the act of holding by attending to two needs. First, it expresses our willingness to pay attention to our children, and we may even sense what they need listening to our heart and the messages it picks up from their hearts. Second, it shows them that we can bear their discomfort – that they do not need to pretend to be good, quiet, brave and so on.

One of the most gracious gifts to offer our children is to let them be themselves, while simultaneously teaching them what is dangerous, what is helpful and what is needed (food or drink or sleep, for example). To deeply connect with our children we must be able to meet them in this moment, for time is an unimportant factor, particularly for pre-school children.

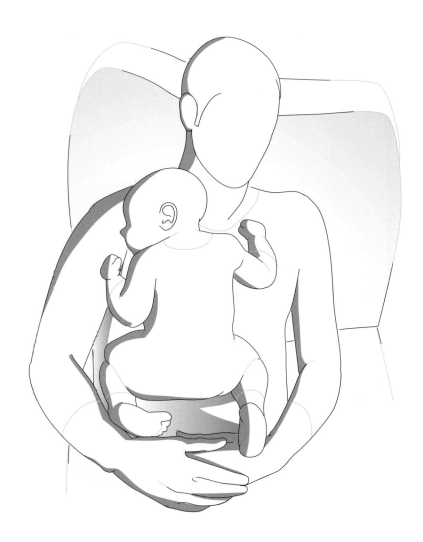

When you play with children, mindfully remember that no goal has to be achieved – the process of building a sandcastle, a Lego town or pretend-biscuits made of Play-Doh is the only thing that matters right now; plus of course the hope that they are enjoying the process and maybe even learning from it.

In the early 20th century Maria Montessori, an Italian psychiatrist, started working with children who were considered underdeveloped in both ability and IQ, often due to living in poverty and not being stimulated. In 1907 she first shared her method with the world. "Help me to do it myself" was one of the main themes of her pedagogic approach. She insisted on letting children evolve in their own time, and attempted to offer tools, toys and materials in classrooms that were totally adapted to children's needs. The furniture, washbasins and toilets were downsized, for example. Adults entered the world of the child, rather than forcing the child to grow up quickly. She had deepest respect for the individuality and personality of each little person. With her revolutionary method, she managed to help children who had been living in mental-health institutions, where they were considered "abnormal", to successfully pass school-leaving examinations.

For me, Montessori totally applied the attitudinal principles of mindfulness and compassion that are discussed in detail in a later chapter: patience, non-judging, acceptance, beginner's mind, trust, kindness and non-striving (see page 288). Her methods are still widely respected, and many Montessori schools exist all over the globe. I sent my children to one such school in Beijing for their infant years and I can highly recommend it.

When I teach mindfulness in pre-school or school, I have noticed that children really have a strong affinity with the Raisin Exercise (see page 64), although we generally use jelly beans. They also deeply enjoy the Body Scan (see page 196), as well as mindful colouring and other creative methods that let them simply "be" and "experiment" with life. They also respond extremely well to compassion-based practices, such as helping another child who is ill or less able with their tasks. And they do not usually expect rewards, if we do not put this idea into their heads.

Children also respect honesty more than we realize. I remember watching Thich Nhat Hanh's movie *Walk with Me*.[5] A little girl comes up to him, crying about the loss of her pet dog. He is very gentle with her, but explains in simple but true words that her dog is now part of the soil, and when it rains and the sun shines onto the wet soil, parts of her dog will float up into the atmosphere and become clouds, which then travel along in the sky until it rains again. The clouds then become rain, fall onto the soil and so the little girl's dog is actually not only in her heart, but everywhere around her.

The little girl totally comprehends the connection that we all have with each other, and that all energy transforms itself but is never lost. Watching Thich Nhat Hanh explaining this to her gave me hope, because if a monk (albeit a very wise and compassionate one) can talk to children and make them understand subjects like loss and death so well, then I am sure a mindful parent will find a way, too.

One of my co-teachers at Entermindfulness is experiencing the wonders and challenges of being a parent to two little ones right now. Monty kindly shared his experience with me and asked, "How can we, as parents, stay mindful?"

Especially in the early years, opportunities for sitting in long periods of meditation are scarce – indeed, our meditation classes are often filled with people who haven't had children yet, or whose children have fled the nest. Being a mindful parent offers an opportunity to experiment with shorter meditations and "on the go" mindfulness, and to unearth subconscious patterns that are brought to life by our parenting. Should you have developed a longer sitting practice prior to parenthood, it is essential to let go of clinging to this particular method and to use everyday parenting as your practice ground.

Without mindfulness, parenting on autopilot can emerge: those times when we act without even realizing – or questioning – what we're doing. Often we find ourselves repeating the same patterns and phrases to our children that our parents used with us – perhaps even aspects that created the very necessity for mindfulness in our own lives in the first place.

How many times have you seen a mother saying to a distressed child, "Try not to worry" or distracting crying toddlers to make them feel better? These are actions born out of love: an effort to shield the child from their pain. And although distractions might work in the short term, in the long term they will teach the child to try and escape painful emotions – rather than accept them and allow them to happen, until sooner or later they resolve.

The following anecdote was shared with me by my co-teacher Monty Cholmeley:

> Right now I am at home, with a four-month-old baby and a four year old. Our eldest hasn't been
> at school for the past three months and, I just learned, won't be allowed back for another three.
> People joked with me that you haven't parented properly until you've had more than one child, but
> no one told me about what to expect when you have a worldwide pandemic at the same time as the
> nappies and late nights.
>
> For me, this has been a time when my mindfulness has saved me; almost daily I have been able to
> catch stress early on, when it is still more subtle — rather than overwhelming and overpowering.
>
> Parenting might be easy without external stressors, but, sadly, life isn't always easy; and when we
> are carrying stress with us, there is less capacity to be patient with our children and to meet their
> needs without snapping — or losing it altogether.
>
> [There] is a practice that I find helpful and use to help me navigate through parenthood. [On the
> following page] is a short meditation to help parents when they're on the brink. You can use it to
> soothe stress when big feelings are present — just go somewhere quiet for a few minutes. Your child
> witnessing you actively managing your stress levels will be an essential lesson for them. Once you're
> familiar with the practice, you can do this in a few seconds or for a few minutes — as long as you
> can manage.
>
> Next time you feel the need to cool down, find a quiet place and try this for a few moments.[6]

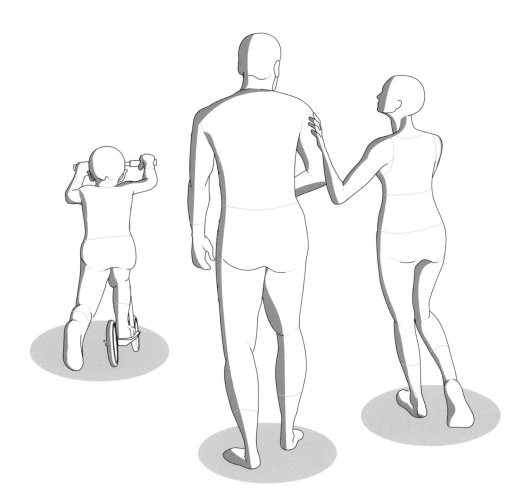

Practice: When Big Feelings Are Present Meditation

Perhaps you are a frazzled parent, or you are stressed for other reasons. Whatever the big feelings, this Body Scan (a key mindfulness practice, see page 196) helps you to mentally locate, acknowledge and release any tension in the body.

Duration: 10 minutes

1. Start by adjusting your posture. You can do this either sitting or standing, while adopting a posture that is relaxed, yet dignified.

2. Gently scanning the body now, become aware of where in the body any noticeable feelings of tension are present: perhaps in the chest, neck or stomach.

3. Don't try to push it away or get rid of it, even if it feels unpleasant. Stay with it, with kindness, welcoming it into your awareness. Be curious to feel all of it, just for now, allowing it to be.

4. Perhaps imagine that, as you breathe in, you feel the difficulty in vivid detail and, as you breathe out, you feel a sense of release, or softening.

5. Breathe in and out of this area as you continue the practice.

6. With a curious attitude, try to really feel the tension in as much detail as you can, getting up close to it. Feel whether it has a shape or a colour.

7. See if you can zoom in right to the point where the feeling is most intense, and then zoom out again, to feel it as a whole. Does it feel like it's vibrating, tingling, tightening or tensing?

8. Even if it feels unpleasant, see if you can be open to it.

9. Finally, bring a sense of compassion to your experience, as if you were comforting a close friend who is suffering. Perhaps put one hand on your cheek, heart or belly and gently say, "It's okay, this is difficult" or "You are welcome here, and I love you." It doesn't matter too much what words you use; simply say whatever it takes to allow the feeling to be heard. You are not trying to change anything or make the feeling go away. Instead you are helping to remove any resistance that you have around the feeling being here. Resisting feelings is tiring, which only makes you feel more exhausted ("What you resist persists!"). Instead, you are experimenting with deepening an attitude of acceptance by using a gentle touch or kind words.

10. As you bring this practice to a close, notice how you are feeling now.

On days when you are so busy you seem to have not even a minute to yourself, you can keep your mind above water by practising mini-mindful check-ins as you go about your day. I like to wash my hands mindfully, exploring the plethora of sensations and temperatures as I scrub them. Or, when walking, you can spend a moment with your focus resting on the sensations you are feeling on your skin: perhaps the warmth of the sun, the cool of a breeze or even the wet of the rain. Experiencing them as they are, without judgement, brings you back to reality, rather than feelings of worry or frustration about the past or the future.

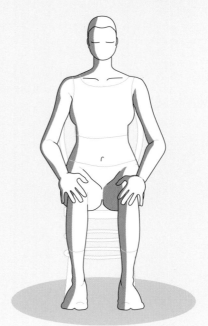

Dealing with Tantrums

When your child is in the middle of a big emotion, expressed either by shouting or by withdrawal, you can use a simplified labelling practice to encourage them gently to name the different emotions they are feeling. (Labelling is a way of breaking down feelings into articulate parts, and it can help a child express emotion.) When I did this with my children, we started amid tears, but after a few times of naming "Angry!" or "Sad!" we began to find the experience funny, and the storm passed.

Finally, if you do lose it, that's okay – you're only human. I've even heard the phrase "If you lose it, you can use it"! Sitting in meditation after your mini-explosion can bring to light many interesting patterns: areas of your own life, perhaps even from your childhood – an inner child that needs some extra attention or its own spot of parenting perhaps.

You might have heard this comment: "Your mental health isn't your fault, but it is your responsibility." Many of our mental hang-ups were unknowingly passed down by our parents (and often their parents before that – and who knows how many generations it's been going on for). When we are young, we learn how to manage our emotions from parents and caregivers. Although it all comes from a good place, these lessons can still leave us unprepared for life, or with options that we would rather not pass on to our little ones.

Mindful parenting gives us a choice. Are we continuing to parent on autopilot, blindly sharing with our children ineffective ways of coping with life's stresses, and cultivating the same bad habits that caused us so much stress and suffering? Or are we going to try and do things differently and stop that cycle forever? With mindfulness, we have the tools to do exactly that.

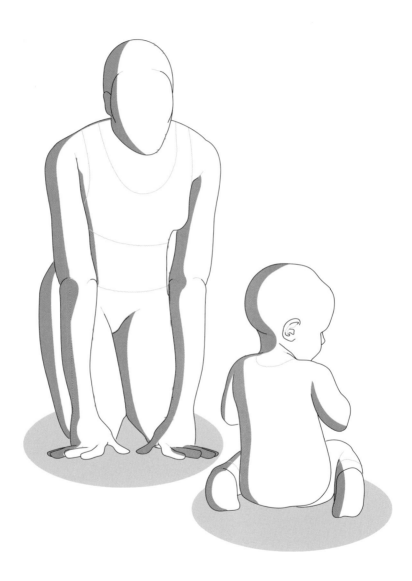

Improving Relationships with All Beings

Whether you want to nourish your connection with little ones, loved ones, friends or workmates, I would like to invite you to practise a few principles as often as you remember them:

- If possible, accept others for who they are, what they wear and their own little foibles.
- Stand or sit in a relaxed way, turning toward other people, so that they feel attended to. Is it possible to focus on their gifts, rather than their flaws?
- If you notice a new piece of clothing, ornament or hairstyle, tell them you like it, if that feels right. If not, just say nothing, unless they ask for an honest opinion.
- Show compassion by offering to help or giving an unexpected gift: "I wish you a very merry unbirthday!" (*Alice in Wonderland*)

Every day, unless we are on a silent retreat, we will probably communicate with others. Are you aware of your own strengths and weaknesses regarding verbal and non-verbal communication? Try your best to be present and to listen to others with attention. Avoid preparing your response before the other person has finished. And watch their body language. What do they really want to tell you? Are they crossing their arms defensively, turning away to create distance or is their body open, and accepting, toward you?

Do you tend to go on a bit, or interrupt others? Or are you, on the other hand, always listening and never contributing? Where could you mindfully find the middle ground? How could you show the other person that you are really paying attention? Eye contact is so important, so that the other person feels heard. A gentle, genuine smile can be such a gift. Smile with both your eyes and your lips.

A Red, Red Rose

O, my luve's like a red, red rose,
          That's newly sprung in June:
O, my luve's like the melodie,
          That's sweetly play'd in tune.

As fair art thou, my bonnie lass,
          So deep in love am I:
And I will luve thee still, my dear,
          'Till a' the seas gang dry.

'Till a' the seas gang dry, my dear,
          And the rocks melt wi' the sun:
And I will luve thee still, my dear,
          While the sands o' life shall run.

And fare thee weel, my only luve!
          And fare thee weel a-while!
And I will come again, my luve,
          Tho' it were ten thousand mile.

– Robert Burns, Scottish poet (1759–1796)[7]

Mindfulness for Mental Wellbeing

Mindfulness techniques have been proven to offer both mental and physical benefits. Research has shown that mindfulness can be linked to decreased levels of the stress hormone cortisol, suggesting that it may also decrease the risk of diseases that arise from stress, such as psychiatric disorder, high blood pressure and migraine. It also suggests that mindfulness can improve sleep (see page 164) and reduce chronic pain and gastrointestinal irritations like peptic ulcers. It is widely used as an additional intervention for treating depression, anxiety, shame and other conditions.

Meditation can also help with healing addictions. Several studies refer to mindfulness activating the self-control regions of the brain. One study shared that smokers who learned mindfulness were more likely to stop smoking by the end of the training (MBCT or MBRP: Mindfulness-Based Relapse Prevention) and at the 17 weeks follow-up.[1] This may be because you can learn "to ride the waves of craving nicotine" until they pass. This is true for other addictions, too. If you can accept the discomfort of the craving and "breathe through it", you may be able to let go of many addictions.

One of the most important insights in respect of mental health is the tendency of our brain to *create negative automatic thoughts* almost continuously throughout our waking hours. These NATs can trigger different destructive emotions in our life experience. The same thought – for example, "Everything I do goes wrong" – can cause one person to feel anxious, another person angry and a third person depressed. So before we start looking at mindful interventions to stop NATs happening quite so often and, even more importantly, not to believe in them any longer unless we have really checked out their validity, it is important to familiarize ourselves with the most common ones.

Here are a few typical NATs that we may have developed while growing up, and which are often a source of unhappiness. They lie just beneath our surface of awareness. Familiarize yourself with them. Once you recognize them, they will slowly become less automatic and less "true" for you. You may become so mindful that one day you are able to say to yourself, "Ah, it's you again. I know you – get lost!"

- I do not fit in anywhere at all
- I am a waste of time
- I will never succeed
- No one can feel as bad as I do
- I am totally unreliable
- I cannot do this any longer
- Life is so unfair
- My life is going nowhere
- Nothing feels fun anymore
- I have had enough
- There is something deeply wrong with me
- I hate myself, and everybody else too
- I wish I could just vanish
- I am a failure
- I feel so hopeless

Anxiety and Fear

Anxiety has often been called an "infectious disease" as it can easily spread from one manifestation to another. Here's an example. I have often treated people experiencing travel anxiety. It may have started on a plane, when the flight was a little rough. You may have felt stuck and out of control. Then you avoid planes and instead have to travel by train, bus or Underground. Imagine now that a train gets stuck in a tunnel … Once again there is no way out and you feel dark, hot and "imprisoned", so you stop these forms of transport too – soon you may have to walk or pay for cabs, which is out of the question on a regular basis, at least for most of us. So a fear that might have started with a random rumble in the air has now spread and stopped you from travelling altogether. Your life is stuck; you may even have to give up your job, particularly if you work on the 15th floor and can't stand being shut in a lift, either.

Does any of the above sound familiar? What we know about anxiety is that the less stress you experience in your life, and the more time you spend in your parasympathetic nervous system (also called the "rest and digest" system – it slows down the heart rate, for example, and encourages the body to relax), the more room for manoeuvre you have, before anxiety takes over your life. I will explain later how mindfulness practice (both formal and informal) can help you do just that. First, let's look at the origins of stress.

"Fight or Flight" Response

Today most of our natural predators have been eliminated because humans live in modern housing, far away from wild beasts. However, modern life has created new triggers. Our pressures now come from ever-changing technology, overpopulation, long commuting times on crowded modes of transport, extended working hours and trying to be superhumans who are good at everything. We frequently leave our places of origin – our tribes, who give us comfort – and are thus more exposed to perceived threats.

Our threat-detection system (the amygdalae in the brain) seems to respond to these new triggers no differently than it responded to wild beasts. A few anxious thoughts and several short breaths are enough to activate the whole "fight, flight, freeze" reaction – the so-called stress response. Our sympathetic nervous system is activated when we interpret a situation as being potentially dangerous, and this is a totally automatic response. It starts sending messages to the adrenal glands, which increase our heart rate, blood pressure, pupil dilation and body temperature, send extra blood to some muscle groups, speed up our breathing and adapt our

digestion. So anxious people may feel nauseous or need to run to the bathroom, because our bodies want to eliminate any undigested food. This frees up the energy normally used for digesting for fighting or running away. It makes us lighter.

Difficult phone calls, demanding relatives or clients – any or all of these can trigger this "fight or flight" response. Short-term activation is what nature created so that we could act promptly and deal with any threat, but the body is not equipped to deal well if this response keeps being switched on in the long term (which may be the case if you can't get along with a demanding boss, for example). This will lead to depletion (burnout) and disease, such as a weakened immune system, which leads in turn to other problems, from the common cold to high levels of acidity, gastrointestinal problems, heart disease, high blood pressure, muscle aches, sleep disruption and even cancer.

Before we look at mindful interventions, I want to reflect briefly on the different types of anxiety that psychotherapy differentiates:

- **GAD**: Generalized Anxiety Disorder is a sense of dread that simply does not let you be. You constantly feel that something terrible is about to happen, and this could lead to social isolation and you may never want to leave home.
- **OCD**: Obsessive Compulsive Disorder pushes you to check on things constantly or to experience horrible thoughts again and again (such as "I will attack people on the street with a weapon"). It creates the urge to complete rituals over and over, and if you suffer from an extreme form of OCD – such as having to check all your electric plugs and locks 20 times or so before you can leave the house – you may no longer have enough time to go to work or socialize. It creates another type of prison, like GAD.
- **Phobias**: These are defined as an obsessive preoccupation or fear of a particular thing. To mention just a few (there are so many): arachnophobia refers to an extreme fear of spiders, which may prevent you from going out; social phobia may make it impossible to attend large meetings with others; and claustrophobia refers to a fear of enclosed spaces.

The most extreme forms of anxiety can lead to panic attacks, where you might feel you are going to die or that the world will end at any minute.

Let Anxiety Pass Away

The following story from Dr Karen Neil is a good example of how mindfulness can help you cope with anxiety:

Mindfulness has helped enormously in my management of anxiety, first giving some distance from the symptoms – moving to observing, rather than being caught up in, the turmoil – then enabling me to engage effective strategies. I had already developed a mindfulness practice before going on to train to teach mindfulness to others. This made it possible to travel to London, including a ride on the Tube, which had long triggered panic. Feeling my feet on the floor of the train, my hand on the rail, and the sensations of the breath in my belly made that journey possible.

Arriving at the training venue, I was not in a good state and just wanted to go home. Greeted by a compassionate trainer [Patrizia Collard], I was given the space to go and settle in my room alone, using the skills I had available at that time. I intentionally deepened my breath, trusting in the knowledge that this would gradually reduce the "fight or flight" response. I anchored my attention once more on the rising and falling of my belly, sheltering from the tumultuous thoughts rushing around my head.

Once settled, I was able to join the group and continue with the week-long training retreat, which was to be transformative. Anxiety was again triggered, however, when it came to my teaching being observed. The compassion of the trainer helped me to settle once more, along with feeling the contact of the ground and connecting to my breath. Perhaps the most valuable advice I received was then offered: "You are not your anxiety." I have never forgotten this, and the broadening to see the rest of me, and how I had become defined by anxiety. This was truly liberating and, from that moment, I have gone from strength to strength with much gratitude.

Anxiety has continued to lessen over the years, by continuing to meditate on a regular basis, allowing anxiety to be present, rather than attempting to fight against it or avoiding situations known to trigger it. We know that avoidance feeds anxiety, and that gradual, compassionate exposure to difficult situations is important. How much I would have missed, had I not faced that challenging Tube journey. I returned for many more courses, and eventually became so relaxed on the Tube that I nearly fell asleep and missed my stop! I also started to enjoy public speaking, having previously had a variety of teaching roles, which I found rewarding but painful.

It is important to note that mindfulness is not solely responsible for my recovery but has led to greater understanding and clarity, the ability to make wiser choices and engage in skilful action to reduce anxiety. Treatment with anxiolytic [anxiety-inhibiting] medication, reducing caffeine and alcohol consumption have been important, together with connection with others, music and nature and, essentially, regular physical activity. Walking in nature with good friends is a favourite, and during a particularly stressful time a nudge from my dear sister to go running was incredibly helpful.

Mindfulness is often misunderstood, and I recommend anybody to give it a second or third chance with a different teacher, before deciding it's not for you. Thinking of it as awareness — allowing us to see clearly "what is", and what we can change — can be a good place to start.[2]

Mindfulness and Self-compassion for Dealing with Anxiety

The regular practice of mindfulness can help you become more aware of delicate sensations in the body, and therefore feel and be in touch with your internal emotional states. This can lead to a better ability to regulate those emotions. So if, for example, you feel your heart racing and a shortness of breath, you may say to yourself, "Ah, there is anxiety there. I know this. It may be uncomfortable, but it is not dangerous." Then you can deliberately slow down your breathing and ground yourself, by really sensing your feet on the surface you are standing upon. Attempt the Three-step Breathing Space (see page 68) or Mindful Self-compassion Break (see page 212).

Practice: Mindful Walking (1)

This is a wonderful way of letting go of fear and truly experiencing the delightful vehicle that we inhabit: our body. Walking meditation can be done either inside or outside; you need to be certain that the environment you choose is safe and protected, so that you won't hurt yourself. A private garden – however small it is – makes an ideal walking spot, but a corridor or a living room can be just as useful. All you need to be able to do is walk ten steps or so in one direction.

Walking meditation is not about getting anywhere, but is rather about bringing awareness to the fact that you are here, in your gently moving body.

Duration: 10–20 minutes

1. First, take a stance, really feeling connected to the Earth, with your feet hip-width apart and very solidly rooted to the ground. Before you start walking, really observe the area you are intending to walk in, always keeping your eyes open and looking straight ahead, not down. Very slowly start to lift your right foot from the ground. Notice the heel peeling off the ground and your weight simultaneously shifting into the left leg and foot.

2. After having peeled the right heel off, observe how you are moving it forward ever so slowly, shifting the foot and then gently placing it down exactly one step ahead.

3. While you are placing the right foot down, observe the left heel beginning to peel off the ground and your weight shifting back into the right leg. You may feel slightly "wobbly" at first, as you have slowed down the pace so much. What can be helpful is imagining making real footprints into the ground (like walking on a sandy beach). Your awareness will be fully occupied with the "lifting, shifting and placing" of each footstep, and with mindfully observing how your weight shifts from left to right, and back again.

4. When you have done approximately ten steps in one direction, take your time turning around. Observe with curiosity how your hips swirl round very gradually. Before starting your next set of steps, stand once again, mindfully rooted to the ground, just breathing.

You may soon become aware of what a complex, awe-inspiring activity walking is — and what a gift it is too, if you are able to do it. With each passage that you walk, it is possible to feel more and more grounded and safe. Once again let me remind you that each person's experience differs, as you participate in this exercise. Engage with this practice with an attitude of openness and curiosity, returning to a state where, like a child, you are discovering once again how you do this walking: the miracle of moving, of being alive, of not needing to get anywhere, but simply being here, trusting in a practice that has a tradition of more than two and a half thousand years.

Start with mindful walking for about ten minutes initially, and expand it gradually to 20 minutes, should you wish to do so. Remember to note down any observations in your journal. The famous meditation teacher Thich Nhat Hanh reminds us in his teachings to connect deeply with Mother Earth.

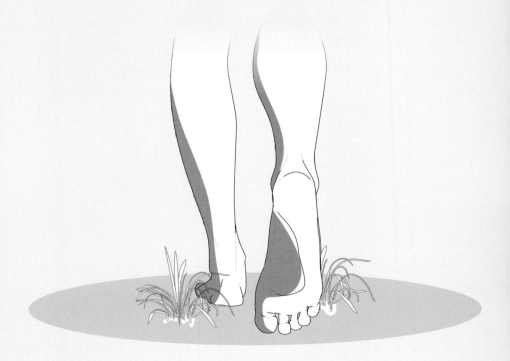

Practice: Guided Walking Journey

Not everyone can walk because of physical or other health challenges. In this case, do a guided journey in the comfort of your home. Like the mindful walking exercise on page 108, this practice brings awareness to the body. You may like to record this journey on your mobile and play it back.

Duration: 10–15 minutes

1. Find a comfortable position: sit in a chair or lie on your bed – if required, prop yourself up with pillows. Close your eyes. Connect with your breath, breathe in and out deeply several times.

2. In your mind's eye (imagination) recall a favourite place outside and in nature. Look at your feet, see them rooted to the Earth.

3. Look up, connect to the space around you. What do you notice about your environment?

4. Spend a few moments creating a picture of the path ahead. The way is easy and clear.

5. Move one foot, then the other. You are walking smoothly, looking ahead. Your body feels at ease as you progress on your path. Walk for as long as you wish.

6. When ready, take a few final deep breaths. Come back to your room, your home.

Summary: How to Feel Less Anxious and More Settled

1. Incorporate regular Mindful Breathing (see page 50) when you start the day, in order to be less susceptible to anxiety. And reread the chapter entitled A Mindful Day (see page 46).

2. In your Mindfulness Journal, write down your EGS (see page 213) regularly before you go to bed and congratulate yourself each time you beat anxiety. "Yes, I can!" should be your motto.

3. Practise the Three-step Breathing Space (see page 68), so that you know it by heart when you need to use it at times when fear seems your closest friend.

4. The Mindful Self-compassion Break (see page 212) is another useful tool.

5. If you feel that people are staring at you, maybe think of something humorous or give yourself a kindly hug.

6. "There is nothing either good or bad, but thinking makes it so!" said Shakespeare's Hamlet in Act 2, Scene 2. Thoughts are not facts – and even if you think something terrible will happen, it rarely does. How often did you not get stuck in that lift, for example? A thousand times or more?

7. Practising the new activities listed above is important. This is the only way to help your "anxious neuropathways" wither and new "brave" ones to grow.

8. Try the Mountain Meditation (see page 124), applying this visualization to your own life. Imagine that even when anxiety seems to be causing you turmoil and you feel you may soon reach the point of panic, deep down within you there is this safe place that you have created through the practice of mindfulness and you can return to it in your mind whenever this seems necessary. (This is why regular practice is paramount.) You could try and visualize any place from a story or a reality where you feel safe and protected.

9. You may prefer the Lake Meditation (see page 125), if you have a stronger affinity to water. Imagine sitting near a beautiful lake.

10. Make peace with your own fears. Part of cultivating mindfulness is accepting "what is". Take ownership of your fears; even if they are a part of you, you are learning to let go of them. For now, they are what they are. Fear is a primal human response to threatening circumstances, and it's essential for our survival. It heightens our senses and helps us protect ourselves. It is an act of self-preservation. Remember: this too will pass.

11. Practise the Connecting With Loss meditation (see page 208).

12. Use some mindful activities to keep yourself calm (see page 220). Here are a few ideas: clear out some clutter; mindfully read some poetry or listen to music that calms your mind; watch the world go by and look out of your window; book a massage and engage in mindful movement and walking.

Having Fun with Sharks – Not for the Faint-hearted!

Real anxiety can of course be triggered by a potentially harmful encounter with a predator. The following is an example of mindful action.

In 2012 my husband and I took part in a dive trip in Viti Levu, Fiji. We were expecting to see tiger and bull sharks, which was the entire purpose of this particular outing. A dive guide started feeding a 5-metre-long (16½-foot-long) tiger shark that was approaching our group. Suddenly, the guide touched its snout and with a quick and unexpected turn, flipped the beast around so that it floated on its back! The shark not only stayed in this position, but also fell into a trance-like state, breathing slowly, roiling its eyes upward and floating peacefully.

While the shark was in this state, the guide touched the shark's belly, fins, tail ... nothing was a no-go zone! This shark was like a tame kitten, as long as its snout was being tended to. After five minutes or so had passed, the guide gently pushed the shark away and it swam off into the deep blue.

It's amazing what a mindful approach can achieve – it may even stave off a real, rather than a perceived, threat – although it's obviously not advisable to rely solely on mindfulness in a high-risk situation. I hope you can mindfully decide how far (or not) you want to explore life's challenges. Free climbing and parachuting are not for everybody. Being "sensible" or "careful" is quite different from suffering from an anxiety disorder.

Depression

Have you ever met "the black dog" of the soul, or is he perhaps a frequent visitor to your house? Depression often occurs after long periods of stress or anxiety, and these conditions can even present themselves simultaneously (known as "comorbidity" in psychological terms). There are certain symptoms of depression that are common, while others seem unique to each individual.

When I experienced my first episode I was around 21. Suddenly the world looked less bright, and colours were pastel rather than vibrant. On the one hand, I felt anxious and had a recurrent dream telling me that I would die at the age of 32; that started my anxiety about falling asleep. I also felt listless – nothing could really excite me, and I felt unattractive and unloved. Life seemed pretty pointless. I would not have minded if it had stopped right then, but I was not actively suicidal.

Here are a few thoughts about depression:
- There are forms of mild depression that last a few hours or days, clinical depression, which lasts for at least two weeks or a few months, and dysthymia, a mild, long-term depression – usually lasting two years or more.
- Depression varies from person to person. When I used to get the blues in my twenties, it usually began with a sense of low mood or sorrow about something I had read in the paper or seen on television, or even just something I experienced in my own life, such as seeing a dead ladybird on the floor. Then I became less and less engaged in life, I stopped answering phone calls, emails, text messages and so on. I also stopped bathing and my hygiene went down the drain. I hung out in my pyjamas for days, I avoided going out. My appetite changed; either I stuffed myself or starved. I began to hate myself, to hate life, to hate everything; I no longer cared whether I lived or not.
- Women seem to be more affected by depression than men.
- Clinical depression has surged to epidemic proportions in recent years. In 2015 the World Health Organization reported that 4.4 per cent of the world's population suffered from depression, an 18.4 per cent increase in the number of people living with depression between 2005 and 2015.[3]
- Once you are depressed, you will tend to have more NATs (see page 100) than the average person, and will be more likely to suffer further episodes in the future. They're like "cold sores of the mind": once you are infected, they can break out throughout your life. Each episode of depression increases by 16 per cent the chances that the person will experience another episode.
- The highest suicide risk is among separated, divorced or recently widowed people who are suffering from depression.

- Another new finding is that people as young as 14 can fall prey to this mental disorder, although they are often thought of as "difficult teenagers" rather than being referred to an appropriate medical professional.
- A new theory is that people who were previously depressed may relapse more easily if there is a deficiency of serotonin – the body's natural "feel-good chemical" – in their brain. This may suggest that depression could be a physical, not a mental, illness. However, sceptics of this theory claim it has been pushed forward by pharmaceutical industries that wish to increase people's dependency on SSRIs, a type of antidepressant that increases levels of serotonin within the brain.
- Other commonly agreed causes of depression are past unresolved trauma or abuse; a genetic predisposition toward it; financial problems; chronic pain or long-term illness.
- Another reason for the ongoing rise in depressive illness has to do with people living longer; 60- to 74-year-olds are more likely to suffer than other age groups, due to a perceived lack of purpose in their lives and the experience of social isolation once they reach retirement age.
- There is a school of thought that states that severe stress or certain illnesses can trigger an excessive response from the immune system, causing inflammation in the brain, which in turn causes depression.
- Finally, high and frequent use of alcohol and other drugs, such as cannabis, ecstasy and heroin, can also play havoc with the brain and cause low mood.

In order to receive a diagnosis of clinical depression you must have experienced a minimum of five or more of the following symptoms for two weeks or longer:

- Depressed/very low mood/becoming upset "for no specific reason"
- Suicidal thoughts – just wanting to disappear into thin air
- Feelings of guilt/worthlessness/anxiety/irritability
- Loss of interest and pleasure
- Difficulty concentrating or remembering
- Insomnia or hypersomnia (sleeping for much longer than usual)
- Decrease/increase in weight/comfort eating
- Tiredness in general or upon waking/loss of energy
- Inability to concentrate/indecisiveness
- Withdrawal from the world around you
- Feeling a sense of dread first thing in the morning
- Loss of desire for intimacy
- Sense of feeling there is no hope or purpose for the future

How to Use Mindfulness to See the "Light at the End of the Tunnel"

Until the early 2000s Cognitive Behavioural Therapy (CBT) was the main treatment for depression. The main objective was to help patients notice their NATs (negative automatic thoughts, see page 100) and challenge them, or replace them with more helpful – and usually more realistic – ways of thinking. MBCT (see page 8) researched how mindfulness could also teach sufferers not to challenge these thoughts, but simply observe them as mental events (true, not true or partially true). We can learn to see NATs as no more than sounds that we may hear or smells that we may smell: coming and going, and impermanent. This really takes the power out of those NATs, for sure!

Practice: Sitting with Your Thoughts (1)

This mindful intervention helps you to separate yourself from your thoughts. Your thoughts are not you – they come and go. By observing your thoughts you create distance from them, helping you to be less affected by the mind's debris. In essence, through this practice you can learn to manage the mind's chatter and find points of stillness.

Duration: 15–20 minutes

1. Go to your allocated meditation place and get into a comfortable and dignified position. Now start this practice by focusing on being really grounded, feeling your feet on the floor and your sitting bones on the chair. Then start to focus on your breathing. Allow it to continue as usual, and bring your awareness to your breath as your anchor of attention.

2. When you experience a sense of settling or even calmness, say to yourself thoughtfully, "Let me see you, Depression – let me remember you in all your details. You are already here for now. I want to get to know you!" (Choose your own words, as appropriate.)

3. Now just keep breathing, and perhaps notice information arising in your awareness – it could be single words, sentences, feelings, sensations, colours or shapes. When information arises, simply notice it and let it pass by, like a bird flying into the sky and out of your mind.

4. You may prefer to use other metaphors to stand behind "the waterfall of your depression". Hold a bunch of balloons, write the information that arises in your mind onto each one of them and then let them go up into the sky – the universe. If you have more affinity to water, you could imagine standing on a bridge, seeing leaves flow by on the water and seeing your insights about depression written on some of the leaves: here one moment, gone the next. If you feel playful right now, you could imagine blowing soap bubbles into the air: each bubble contains a thought, an insight; it floats away and then bursts. Gone! The main objective is to see how impermanent these negative thoughts or emotions are, coming and going. And this is really important: They are not you!

5. After a while, when information starts to repeat itself or stops, return to your breath as your anchor of awareness, until you decide to end this meditation.

Journaling

Once again, writing down your experience can be therapeutic. Note down all the information you gained through the exercise on the previous page. Once you get going, you may possibly remember even more details about how depression manifests itself in your life and your experience. As we are all different and unique, there may well be several aspects that I have not mentioned in the list of symptoms on page 116 that are typical for your experience of the "shadowy night of the soul". Furthermore, you could note down how variable each day and each hour of your life with depression can be.

Have you noticed any changes in your sleeping or eating patterns? Or anything else that you typically like doing, but have now stopped doing? Maybe you want to give your symptoms a name – perhaps even a funny one. It can be helpful to bring some lightness into this "dark cave".

Practice: Pleasant-event Diary

This practice is a wonderful way of bringing awareness to the little joys and miracles that happen daily; the kinds of things that aren't obvious to us because we do not readily pay attention to such small moments. Here are some examples of pleasant experiences, but do be creative and observe your very own marvels that life presents you with: seeing new shoots or blooms in an unexpected place; a lovely sound in your environment; a kind gesture by a stranger or a loved one; eating something that tastes out of this world; or being really satisfied with something you managed to do.

Duration: 5–20 minutes

1. On a blank page in your journal, write down the days of the week, allowing space to record your experiences each day.

2. Every day, ask yourself the questions below and record your answers in your journal. Write down at least one experience per day, although more would be even better.
   - What was the experience?
   - Were you aware of the pleasant feelings while the event was happening?
   - How did your body feel, in detail, during this experience?
   - What moods, feelings and thoughts arose during this event?
   - What thoughts and feelings are you aware of now, as you write this down?

Other Practices to Reduce Depression

- **Mindful Breathing** (see page 50): The breath is always there, and so you can access it without too much trouble. After the exercise, write down in your journal what thoughts came up, what you noticed and how you are feeling after having done this.
- **(Fast) Mindful Walking**: In order to activate yourself, and to reduce the tiredness and lethargy caused by depression, you could try and experiment with fast Mindful Walking (see page 108). Find a spot where you can walk swiftly about 30–50 steps forward. First stand upright, with your feet hip-width apart, grounding yourself by sensing three points of contact (heel, big toe and little toe), letting your shoulders hang loosely and keeping your head and spine upright. Let your gaze focus on one spot ahead; refrain from looking down at your feet. Now start walking with vigour. Your anchor of awareness is each step, which you could visualize as a footprint on the ground. Also focus on your breathing, noticing its intensity rising with each round you have completed. Do this for about 20 minutes, walking forward and backward energetically.
- **Brief Body Scan**: Read the instructions for the full Body Scan (see page 196). However, this time I am inviting you to sweep swiftly through your body. I mean that you should pay less detailed attention to each body part than in the full Body Scan; instead, breathe into your body with intention and imagine a strong gust of wind sweeping through you. Experiment a little. I find that in this way the Body Scan becomes more active and invigorating, while at the same time you are still attending to yourself with kindness and patience.
- **Yoga for a peaceful mind**: Yoga connects you to the body and helps you to find stillness within; all the poses have different qualities. Kindly try the Mountain Pose (see page 122) and also Yoga to Find Your Centre (see page 246).

Practice: Mountain Pose

This yoga pose strengthens your legs, improves posture and may help you feel like a strong mountain.

Duration: about 5 minutes

1. Start by standing with your feet hip-width apart. Your arms should be dangling down by your sides, with the palms facing in, gently touching the thighs.

2. Now breathe in a few times and bring awareness to your breathing. When you are exhaling, contract the pelvic-floor muscles and lift them up until you feel a squeeze at the base of your buttocks – a physical sensation as if your sitting bones are coming closer together. This action supports the spine from below.

3. Continuing to breathe evenly, on the next exhalation draw the entire abdominals toward the spine and at the same time lengthen the spine upward. Stand tall, with the spine erect and the head lifted.

4. Breathe in deeply, creating with each in-breath a sense of space in the entire chest area. On the exhalation roll the shoulders up, back and down, releasing any tension that you may be aware of in the upper-back area.

5. Stand here and, with each in-breath, feel a lifting up in the entire spine; and with each out-breath, as you gently draw the naval to the spine, feel the support you are giving to your lower back. Practise this for about five minutes.

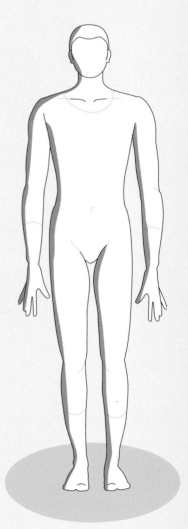

Practice: Mountain Pose with Arms Up

This is an extension of Mountain Pose for those people who have no tension in their shoulders.

Duration: about 5 minutes

1. Stand in Mountain Pose (see opposite). Breathe in and, on the out-breath, stretch your arms downward.

2. On the next inhalation, lift your arms out to the sides, fingers pointing toward the ceiling. Continue and, if this feels comfortable, slowly move your arms and hands over your head until the palms of the hands are facing each other. The arms should be in a V–shape or slightly closer, shoulder-width apart; or by the sides of the ears, with the palms touching each other.

3. With every exhalation see if you can gently roll the shoulders back and down, and with every inhalation try to stretch the arms a little bit more. When you can't move any more, hold the position for three to five in- and out-breaths.

4. Then gently return to lengthening the spine, turning the palms outward so that the backs of the hands are touching each other.

5. On the exhalation, start to move the arms out to the sides, then back and down. Move slowly until your back is once again in the starting position.

6. Repeat this exercise three to five times.

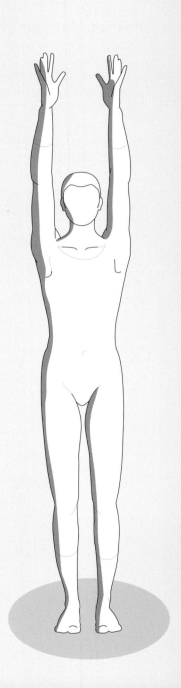

Practice: Mountain Meditation

While doing the Mountain Pose (see page 122), you may feel inspired to visualize a beautiful strong mountain: one you have seen in real life, in a picture or movie, or one you have just created in your imagination. Stand with a strong stance for a few mindful rounds of breathing in and out, and maybe even "become" the mountain!

If you prefer to sit, you can still access the benefits of the grounding Mountain Pose. Sit on a chair with both feet on the ground and your back straight. Let your hands rest on your thighs.

Duration: 5 minutes

1. Breathe slowly, find stability through your breath.

2. Imagine being a mountain; you are solid, rooted to the Earth.

3. The weather around the mountain may vary. Sometimes it is pleasant and sunny, however, suddenly, the sky fills with dark clouds. Soon rain is pouring down; the trees are bending because of the powerful wind. However, you, the mountain, are still during the storm. You are calm, you are peaceful.

4. Take a few final deep breaths. The mountain's stillness and peace are abiding, and within you.

Practice: Lake Meditation

Like the Mountain Meditation (see opposite), you can do this practice standing or sitting.

Duration: 5 minutes

1. Imagine sitting near a beautiful lake. The water appears in shades of blue and green, the surface is calm.

2. You are encircled by expansive mountains. Colourful flowers grow near your resting spot. The sounds of birds and insects hum around you.

3. The water of the lake smells fresh, you notice the soft touch of a breeze. You feel at peace, you feel tranquil.

4. Now, you notice that deep down in the lake there is another world; it is calm and beautiful.

5. You can return to this beautiful lake whenever you wish to enjoy its tranquillity.

Making Time, Not Finding Time

Even when you feel low, this is your life, and you have to take responsibility for making time to take care of depression – your mind and body are very important and shouldn't take second place behind other things. You can't function properly without looking after yourself, so don't take yourself for granted or think that overcoming this obstacle is not as important as your work, for example. Read the chapter Finding Joy and Mindful Activities (see page 220), or remember things you used to do that made you happy and joyful.

Sometimes showing compassion toward others who are suffering can take you out of your own mind and help you feel useful, with a sense of purpose. Perhaps you can visit a place for the homeless, the elderly or forsaken pets. Offer a few hours of your time to work there free of charge. Your reward will be the smiles of the residents or gentle purring of the creatures you just helped.

The Man Who Was "Eaten Up" by Guilt

When he arrived in my office for his first session, Jack was beside himself. A man in his late forties, he was telling me about the recent weeks of his life and how he had brought it all upon himself: redundancy and not being offered a good reference for a new job, as he had left numerous important projects undone, simply hiding them in a drawer. He had been working for a small charity, and nobody used computers much at that time.

He said he had considered killing himself, as there was no way forward – not at his age, not without a reference, and anyhow he deserved no better! He moved between anxiety, depression and anger. He suddenly jumped up, yelling massive self-abuse at himself, rushed toward my windows and pulled down the curtains in order to release this extreme rush of emotions. My colleagues knocked hard on my door and kept asking whether I was all right. I said I was able to handle the situation. Jack was not a bad or aggressive man; he just felt he had fallen into this deep black hole and was without trust of ever finding a way out.

As he was so emotionally aroused, simple CBT would not have sufficed. I gently touched both of his shoulders and kindly asked him to sit down. We then started to focus on feeling his feet on the ground, and to connect to his breathing. I was almost whispering, breathing, "In and out, in … out", and then I used the loving-kindness words of metta meditation, which is a form of self-compassion meditation: "May you be safe and protected, may you be peaceful, may you live at ease and with kindness, feeling safe, protected, peaceful, at ease" and so on. Almost like a lullaby, breathing with him, repeating the words and sending him deep-felt kindness from my heart.

After about 20 minutes Jack started to calm down and, alongside the breathing, he had silent tears flowing down his cheeks into his big beard. He was shaking a little, but soon this also stopped. This was the beginning of a long journey of self-discovery, self-compassion and forgiveness. Jack continued coming for one-to-one therapy for about a year, and thereafter for many years to my monthly meditation evenings. Mindfulness and compassion helped him to start afresh. And I happen to know that he is still doing well.

Free

Let the ocean's waves enwrap you gently,
Gazing forth –
the glimmer of the moon.
The heavy load of life
Leave far behind you
And listen deeply
To the music of your heart.
Never to be touched again
By pain or suffering
Enjoy the peace
Henceforth –
Be still, be free!

– Patrizia Collard

PTSD

PTSD, Post-Traumatic Stress Disorder, is catalysed by exposure to an extremely traumatic event, such as witnessing or hearing about an event that involved death, injury or a threat to oneself or to someone else. This chapter looks at how mindfulness practices can be used to work for people with PTSD, with a special focus on traumatized veterans.

When I worked as a senior lecturer at the University of East London, I supervised numerous research studies based on mindfulness. One that was particularly thought-provoking was working with a therapist who was helping war veterans overcome traumatic experiences, with the help of mindfulness-based interventions. In the discussion below I will summarize the findings that she shared with me. And I invite anybody who is experiencing PTSD to try some of the mindfulness-based programmes that are offered for this specific emotional disorder.

Caution: If you suffer from long-term, deep trauma it may be best to undertake this work with an experienced therapist. I would advise against using apps and other quick mindfulness fixes, and suggest that you do some research to find an appropriate counsellor or course to attend.

As mentioned previously, mindfulness involves cultivating an attitude of "acceptance" of moment-by-moment experiences. Therefore it was particularly helpful to discover that mindfulness-based treatments were supportive to a client group who were stereotypically avoidant of seeking help.

For example, in 2012 David J Kearney et al. made research outcomes available that indicated that in a group of veterans in the US, Mindfulness-Based Stress Reduction (MBSR) "shows promise" as an intervention for PTSD.[4] What is commonly known when treating veterans with PTSD is their reluctance to pursue therapy, believing themselves to be "weak", feeling shame (see the section on shame on page 138) and fearing social stigma. They usually suffer in silence.

One very interesting example is the story of "The Railway Man". Eric Lomax experienced his personal trauma during the Second World War, and yet he only published his autobiography in 1995, some 50 years later.[5] And before he died, in 2012, he was able to assist in the making of the film based on his experience.[6] It vividly describes his challenges as a prisoner of war when he was forced to help build the Thai–Burma Railway for the Japanese military. Among other events, he was force-marched to the notorious prison camp at Changi, and was tortured for "anti-Japanese activities" when a secret radio was found in the camp. His story moved me deeply, because it is unbelievable what human beings are capable of doing to one another, and how the human spirit can survive such appalling experiences. In *The Railway Man* Lomax learns, through loving and trusting his second wife Pattie, finally to re-engage with the beauty that life can offer.

As a volunteer for Amnesty International in my twenties, I had come across victims of torture and trauma before, so it was my particular wish to become the supervisor for the aforementioned study, for it combined my interest in both the alleviation of trauma and the use of mindfulness in overcoming it.[7] Even when working for Amnesty, I had noticed that some Buddhist monks who had been tortured tended to experience less trauma than many other victims of torture. Could it be that their practice of mindfulness meditation somehow strengthened their mind and heart? One possible explanation was their deep and extensive practice of compassion-based meditation. If you feel deeply sorry for your torturer, for he has to live with his crimes against humanity, then you may feel more sorrow for his pain than for your own, and thus experience less trauma.

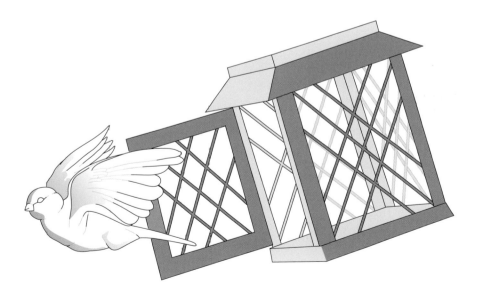

According to a study by N S Scheiner (2008), it can be very challenging to find appropriate treatment by clinicians who are confident in, and experienced at, meeting the specific needs of people traumatized in combat.[8] Veterans anecdotally report feeling misunderstood and mistrustful of civilian mental-health services.

In the United States, health services for veterans have been well developed for a while; Anka Vujanovic et al. (2011) report that most of the Veterans Health Administration centres in that country suggest some form of mindfulness treatment as part of the programme of treatment.[9] This was a welcome bit of information that helped our project to go forward.

The three typical symptoms that define PTSD are "re-experiencing", "avoidance" and "hyper-arousal":
- "Re-experiencing" encompasses repeated and distressing memories about the event: images, thoughts, nightmares and hallucinations.
- "Persistent avoidance" of these distressing reminders can, over time, lead to a narrowing down of experiencing life (this is exceptionally well described in Lomax's book *The Railway Man*).
- "Increased arousal" can lead to difficulty in falling or staying asleep, irritability or outbursts of anger; difficulty in concentrating; and hyper-vigilance.

All veterans who attended my students' intensive six-week treatment programme (based on MBSR/MBCT programmes) had a dual diagnosis of PTSD with a comorbid diagnosis of depression (see the section on Depression on page 114). Those veterans who engaged regularly during the course, and then practised at home with determination, were able to develop an increased ability to observe not only themselves, but also how they related to others. By being more aware of the present moment, they could dampen down their impulsive and often exaggerated defence reactions toward others, and respond with an increased sense of personal choice to start interacting with other human beings once more. Furthermore, they learned to appreciate and connect to others with less fear and a greater sense of adventure (new life!).

Here are the main themes that the veterans were introduced to during our study and invited to develop their practice around:

- **Opening up to the process of developing mindfulness, and thereby opening up to life**: Getting involved in the process, when possible applying self-discipline, overcoming obstacles, changing step-by-step, becoming natural, continuing self-efficacy, choice, noticing, impulse control, non-judgement, self-regulation, overcoming non-engagement and increased confidence.
- **Responding to PTSD symptoms**: Non-reactivity to inner experience, coping with negative thinking, sadness and anniversaries.
- **Sleep**: Hyper-arousal, anger, hyper-vigilance, anxiety. When an individual is anxious, they may experiences alertness, raised heart palpitations and an increase in adrenaline. This makes it much more difficult to let go of thinking, in particular of negative thinking, and the individual becomes restless and unable to fall asleep. Hyperarousal defines a state of being on high alert, almost ready for an attack or expecting something terrible to happen. This is very typical for veterans or even civilians in war situations. Sleep, if it comes at all, is superficial, never deep. Adrenaline and lack of sleep will eventually also lead to mood swings, often to aggressive behaviour in situations around combat.
- **Reappraisal of threat**: Sense of self in the world, staying present with the self, increased wellbeing, the possibility of a spiritual reality existing, reparation, calmer, inner peace, inner safety, inside energy, connectedness, relationships and appreciation.

In addition my student found that if mindfulness had such an important impact on her client group of veterans suffering from PTSD, then this should have implications for the training programmes of upcoming psychotherapists.

Looking at the many areas of conflict on our globe, and at the huge number of soldiers, veterans and traumatized refugees seeking to find a new home in the West, it strikes me as increasingly necessary to train therapists in Mindfulness-Based Interventions for those who have experienced trauma in war zones, natural catastrophes and new challenges such as pandemics.

New Study

An interesting research study was carried out with active-duty soldiers, who tend to experience highly stressful mental and emotional demands, which can lead to mental exhaustion. Recently, professional military trainers have started offering mindfulness training to soldiers and navy personnel, having adapted it to this client group.

The psychologist and mindfulness educator Dr B Grace Bullock writes about a study reported in Mindful magazine in February 2020 discussing MBAT (Mindfulness-Based Attention Training), which offers insight into training military professionals in this specialized approach.[10] The study was a controlled one, where different groups were exposed to different methods. Group One was trained in MBAT by military trainers who had no prior experience of meditation before attending a 12-week training course. They learned mindfulness-based meditations for several weeks, which was immediately followed by teacher training – that is, how to teach this to soldiers thereafter. Group Two was trained by teachers with prior mindfulness teacher-training experience, but no history of working with soldiers. 180 on-duty male US Army soldiers joined one of three groups: Group One, Group Two or a third group that did not receive any MBAT training at all.

The programme ran over four weeks and offered two-hour-long sessions weekly to the first two groups. This included mindfulness meditations such as the Body Scan (see page 196), concentration practices and learning to connect more deeply to the present moment. The home practice required the soldiers to meditate at least four times per week (for 15 minutes at a time). All participants from the three groups filled in questionnaires prior to, and after, the four weeks were completed.

The surprising outcome was that those soldiers trained by military professional trainers practised more diligently than those with regular mindfulness teachers. The familiarity and knowledge these military trainers had of what life was like as a soldier seemed to make a difference and was a motivator. As the study reported, "The findings suggest that it is possible to improve accessibility of effective mindfulness training programs for groups like soldiers, firefighters, police officers, ambulance personnel and surgeons."[11] Peers should be trained and then deliver the programme, rather than inviting outside trainers who were unfamiliar with the specific institution. And train-up time could be achieved in as little as 12 weeks.

I wonder, of course, whether a more in-depth training of the "inside trainers" would have led to even better results.

Trauma and shame are often deeply connected. On the one hand, you may feel guilty for being alive, for instance, when others were not so lucky. On the other hand, you may feel shame for not feeling grateful for the gift of life! Once again it is "self-compassion" and "acceptance" that may, with regular practice, gently guide you into freedom from both trauma and shame.

He Wishes for the Cloths of Heaven

Had I the heavens' embroidered cloths,
Enwrought with golden and silver light,
The blue and the dim and the dark cloths
Of night and light and the half-light,
I would spread the cloths under your feet:
But I, being poor, have only my dreams;
I have spread my dreams under your feet;
Tread softly because you tread on my dreams.

– William Butler Yeats, Irish poet (1865–1939)[12]

Shame

"The dark shadow of the Mind!"

– Professor Paul Gilbert, clinical psychologist[13]

The experience of feeling shame is often seen as a very "hidden" emotion. It is frequently found to be the basic underlying sentiment that can lead to anger, fear or low mood, and can at times even assume trauma-like characteristics. Somebody who is experiencing shame frequently avoids being in contact with any shame memories, and this attempt to avoid it causes even more suffering, more tension and more stress. Shame can also lead to eating disorders, social anxiety, depression, OCD (see page 104), phobias, BDD (Body Dysmorphic Disorder) and PTSD (Post-Traumatic Stress Disorder, see page 130).

Negative judgements made about ourselves can include feelings of contempt, disdain or even a sense of ridicule. These emotions are then often externalized, because it seems easier to cope with them this way. We may even transfer them onto others and express anger or aggression toward other people. On the other hand, we may lead a "hidden existence" because we fear that others may be able to read our mind and judge us harshly. This type of negative self-evaluation is often referred to as "internal shame". This tells us how we perceive the value of our own existence – that is, as being bad/flawed/worthless/unattractive. The thoughts that arise are that we are simply not good enough. Our internalized ideal or standard is often far too high and often cannot be reached.

Shame is often created by experiences with caregivers in our formative years, such as neglect, aggression, physical or sexual abuse. All tend to have an impact on the development of self-relevant beliefs and identity. Shame has a pervasive influence on emotional "self-regulatory skills" (for instance social avoidance: not wanting to meet people; or even leaving one's home: agoraphobia).

The way this plays out is that you will most definitely not discuss your problems with friends, family members or partners. And without speaking and sharing with others, there is no feedback to tell you that your intrusive thoughts and doubts about yourself are normal. This will lead to an increased sense of isolation, which can contribute to low mood.

From the neurobiological viewpoint, shame is such a powerful emotion that it can trigger the body's shutdown response, just like stress, fear or anger. Feeling shame may affect your whole life. You may protect your body from the feelings associated with shame, experience "freeze'"(no feelings) and even engage in self-harm such as cutting or burning yourself, as this pain seems easier to bear than the feeling of shame. Extreme cases resort to a fourth form of shutdown that we can call "appease". When we act in this mode, we are often in danger of becoming "slaves" to stronger, more aggressive alpha humans. We don't care that we are exploited, because deep down we feel we deserve it.

From a mindfulness perspective, we can ask ourselves, "Where am I feeling shame in the body?" You may notice tension below the diaphragm and a sense of heaviness, as if you are no longer able to move. You may even want to disappear and dissociate (pretend you are no longer there, or feel invisible or not feel your body). You may appear rude to others because you lose your sense of other people, who judge that you are ignoring them. This can then lead to building "associations" in the higher brain, and these are NATs or negative automatic thoughts (see page 100). They are of course deeply connected with the physiological feelings below the diaphragm (a rubbery feeling in the legs, the sense of passing out or wanting to disappear).

Practice: Mindful "Soften/Soothe/Allow" Meditation

This meditation, which uses the breath and awareness, can help to locate points of tension in the body. This meditation aims to release unbalancing shame energy. It is a gentle technique and safe for you to do alone. If you feel emotional afterwards you may find it helpful to chat to a trusted friend or family member. Ask them to listen to your experience without judgement – sharing an emotional burden can often help its power to melt away.

Before you begin, try to remember a mild to moderate shame experience, where you recall feeling a little embarrassment, not too much. If the feelings become intense or uncomfortable, return to awareness of your breath. Consider the following questions, taking a brief pause in between questions:

• How much do you think this memory has influenced your sense of self? (Pause)
• Does it trigger unpleasant emotions or sensations? (Pause)
• Do you find it hinders your enjoyment of life and is operating in the background? (Pause)
• To what extent do you evade thinking about it, or would you like to work on it? (Pause)

Duration: 15–20 minutes

1. Now take a comfortable position, sitting or lying down, covering yourself with a blanket (soothing) and closing your eyes, either a little or completely.

2. Bring your focus to your breathing and put one hand on your chest and one on your abdomen. Notice the gentle inflow and outflow. Repeat this for a few minutes, just connecting to your breathing. Your compassionate self-touch, where you placed your hands, will help you get a sense of being supported by yourself, feeling safer and less alone.

3. Now visualize or remember the situation as a story: maybe you were rude to somebody or ignored somebody who asked for your help. You may never want to share this event with others, but do not select anything that could cause you sleepless nights!

4. Now ask yourself what exactly you are embarrassed about: is it "having felt or expressed anger" or "having acted in a selfish manner"? Can you perhaps name the shame memory: "I am not generous", "I am unfriendly", "I am too frightened" and so on.

5. Gently feel into the depths of your body, seeing whether you can find the area that feels most tender or exposed – you might experience tension or tightness there. Now, if you can, place one hand on this area of your body or mentally attend to it.

6. Allow yourself to soften exactly there, saying to yourself: "Soften, soften, soften", as if you are gently letting go of this tension or discomfort. Once again, if this becomes too challenging or anxiety-provoking at any point, return to the simple breath of life: in and out, in and out. (Pause.)

7. When you are able, kindly say some comforting words to yourself: "May I feel ease or peace" or "Ease, peace, calm", and then the words "Soothing, soothing, soothing".

8. To bring this practice to an end, see if you can find a sense of permission, letting any remaining sense of discomfort in mind or body simply be there. Say to yourself, "Allowing, allowing, allowing". It is what it is, for now. (Pause.)

9. If you would find it helpful, do add another round of softening, soothing and allowing – just the words, repeating them until you begin to feel calmer and more at peace.

10. I want to invite you now to remember that nobody is perfect, and we all make mistakes. Could it be that you are judging yourself too harshly? How would you feel if somebody else had told you the same story? How would you feel about him or her? And remember that thoughts are not facts!

11. Now finish this meditation by gently connecting your feet and other surface points of your body to the ground. Feel deeply rooted and safe, as best you can. You might even want to visualize an image of safety and strength: a big rock, a tree or a mountain. Choose your own image, so that it makes sense for you.

Dealing with Shame

Before I talk further about shame, I would like to emphasize my earlier point that "thoughts are not facts" (see page 111). So, what are thoughts? Thoughts are mental beliefs, ideas and opinions about ourselves and the world around us. We can have worry thoughts, intuitive thoughts, happy thoughts, sad thoughts, depressive thoughts, the list is endless. Thoughts about ourselves are often formed by our life experiences, while thoughts about self-identity can be shaped by our childhood. Alas, negative messages from an elder or carer are often believed and deeply etched into our memory. "Shame" thoughts are among the hardest to shift!

One of the most powerful television series that really focuses on "shame", and how it can destroy people's lives, is called *Broken* and was shown in six parts on British television in 2017.[14] It portrays a Catholic priest, Father Michael Kerrigan, who serves in Liverpool. He has his own demons to battle with, having committed some shameful acts in his youth and having experienced a traumatic childhood, too. Due to his complete promise of silence, he can listen and absolve others, who feel shame about their actions.

In one episode, an unemployed mother of three kids does not inform the authorities of her mother's death and keeps the body for days, so that she can continue receiving her mum's state pension. The priest supports her by listening and by helping when the police get involved. In another episode an accountant comes to Confession, after not having been to church for decades. She shares that she has a gambling addiction, which led her to steal money from her company. She is about to be discovered, after one of the illegal cheques that she signed bounces. She is intending to commit suicide, as the shame of her actions is unbearable for her to live with. Although Father Michael tries his best, she acts on her intentions and leaves her adolescent children behind, who now have to live with her shame and fend for themselves. I found the series very moving and highly accurate in portraying shame in real life – and how destructive it can be.

Another Way of Dealing with Shame

In his book *The Art of Forgiveness, Lovingkindness and Peace*, the Buddhist practitioner Jack Kornfield writes about a radically different way of dealing with shame, which I have summarized below.[15]

Among the Babemba tribe of South Africa, when someone acts irresponsibly, he is made to stand in the centre of the village. All work stops, and everybody in the village gathers in a large circle around the defendant. Then each person speaks to him, one at a time, recalling the good things he has done in his lifetime. Every experience is shared at length – all his positive attributes, his good deeds, his strengths and kindnesses – in a tribal ceremony that often lasts for several days. Afterwards the tribal circle breaks up, a celebration occurs and the accused is welcomed back into the tribe, both symbolically and literally.

Imagine if we could do some version of that for ourselves! Recalling one's good deeds is a classical practice to counteract the tendency toward guilt and shame. You might try this for yourself.

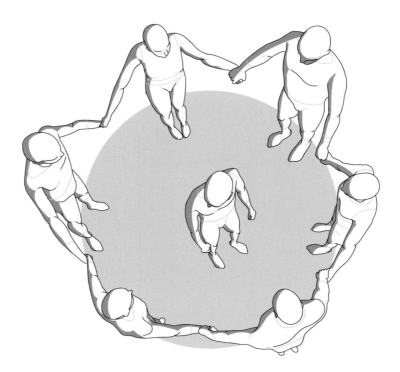

Altaussee Lake

Early morning mist covering
the mighty mountains watching
standing guard of little busy folks
two tiny fishing boats meandering
through turquoise deep waters
covering shadows, rocks, grottoes
now nets laid into the depth
sinking through the silver droplets
surfacing the lake like thin lace
gentle sun beams are breaking through
is there anything more enticing?
More beautiful than this moment
Has my mind made this all up?
A postcard from a book
But I am standing on this balcony
I am breathing
I am
It is

– Patrizia Collard

3
FOOD
AND SLEEP

Mindful Eating

We all need to eat. However, food is a very delicate matter, and consuming it mindfully is a challenge in itself. In the West more and more people struggle with some sort of dissonant relationship with food. In the developing countries of our globe, on the other hand, many times there is not enough food available and eating becomes a struggle for survival.

I know, from research and from my own experience, that I am addressing one of the most difficult forms of addiction to rid yourself of. With the right support and a lot of patience and acceptance of lapses, eating poorly can be overcome. The main issue with food is that we need to learn to re-create a wholesome relationship with it. Whether you are eating too much (which may lead to obesity) or too little (anorexia nervosa or bulimia), you cannot simply eradicate food from your daily life. From a psychotherapeutic perspective, anorexia nervosa is one of the hardest mental-health disorders to treat. Some research suggests that it will take a minimum of two years to relearn how to have a wholesome connection with food and your body.

There are numerous new diets that the "weight-management industry" tries to sell to desperate consumers every year, whether it is the blood-group diet, the keto diet (high fat, low carb) or others based on calorie-counting. We often find ourselves eating in autopilot mode. We have lost the tradition of sharing food with others, sitting down together and enjoying with gratitude and mindfulness the gifts we have been blessed with.

I recently watched a television programme on the phenomenon of rich Russian clients being keen on purchasing big, restored 19th-century flats in central Vienna. They love the architecture, the quality of the air and the multicultural scene of the restaurants. They will gladly spend up to four million euros on such a property, and expect luscious bathrooms and wet-rooms and living room/party areas. But they do not care for having a kitchen built in. That room is generally left bare and is used as a storage facility. Their habit is either to go to an expensive restaurant or have excellent ready-made food delivered to their home.

When I visited California a few years ago, the same phenomenon was present – no kitchen or dining tables; maybe a microwave to heat up some leftovers. There were no plates available in the flats we rented for our stay, either. But the reason in the US is the exact opposite to the previous situation in Vienna. It simply is a lot cheaper to get takeaways and eat them right out of the packaging than to buy fresh food and prepare it. I was truly astonished. Of course both stories represent only a sample of the world's population, but for me they show that preparing and eating food as a mindful, tribal activity has, alas, often lost its appeal.

Revolutionize Your Relationship with Food

Frequently we overeat due to stress hormones floating through our body's system. When we experience the "fight or flight" response (see page 102), the body thinks it is in danger and prepares for battle (attack, or getting away and hiding quickly). The body requires quick resources to fuel all the extra tasks it needs to perform (more blood to the extremities, for running or punching harder), more visual focus and more blood to certain brain areas. In order to get that extra fuel, we experience an urge to eat sugar or carbohydrates as they can easily be converted into energy.

Are you getting the picture? If you are stressed a lot, you are not going to have a desire to eat carrots or cucumbers, unfortunately. As we will read in a later chapter, the brain often cannot differentiate between real danger and perceived danger (even watching a thriller can set off the stress response). The body simply does what it evolved to do many thousands of years ago.

Another trigger that lures us into eating more – and not necessarily the right, wholesome stuff – is loneliness, and anxiety about the state of loneliness. We fill up the empty space and feel safer. A gazelle will never graze if a lion is on the prowl. Feeding, for mammals, equals a sense of safety.

A small, yet growing body of research suggests that a slower, more caring way of eating could help with weight problems and retrain us to opt for healthier food choices. And mindfulness can be helpful in learning to differentiate between emotional and physical hunger, by introducing a "moment of choice" (one mindful breath or the Three-step Breathing Space, see page 68) before you eat the first thing you notice in your fridge or cupboard. A study at the University of California that researched obese women found those who followed a mindful eating programme (noticing fullness or taste, for example) along with meditating to reduce anxiety, saw a marked reduction of internal visceral fat (associated with heart disease), compared with those women who didn't follow the programme.[1]

Once you have learned to select the right food (ideally when you are shopping), you can apply mindfulness in deliberately choosing a smaller plate and eating nourishing fresh food, rather than a packet of potato chips or biscuits. If you then learn to eat each mouthful as a separate action (each breath is a unit of its own, like eating one tiny raisin mindfully in the Raisin Exercise on page 64), you can retrain yourself to eat more slowly and to recognize the signs of satiety. You may wish to start with one meal a week, then one meal a day, and eventually learn to eat

most meals in a more mindful manner. The goal of eating more mindfully should not only be weight loss, but also general health, overall wellbeing, a sense of calm and a lack of compulsion.

However, what we are up against are not only our own unhelpful behaviours, but ancient neuropathways in our human brains. These evolved over a long time to help us survive:

- Our bodies were adapted for energy conservation (put on weight quickly, don't lose it easily). I would have done well thousands of years ago, as I would have been among those who survive a period of starvation.
- Humans were made to "see food and eat it".
- We were built to eat as fast and as much as possible (it takes about 20 minutes for the signal that "enough is enough" to reach the brain circuits).

Furthermore, so many of us no longer have a loving, respectful relationship with our body. Only film stars always look great, often because they have helped "mother nature" by paying a good surgeon to make everything look perfect. Many ordinary human beings dislike their looks, feel unattractive and wish they looked different. It used to be mainly women going under the knife to improve their body image, but lots of men are also doing so now.

The body has needs that have to be met, such as sleep, drink, food and movement. The mind has desires, and we need to deal with them skilfully. When we are on autopilot, we feel we want this food – there is no other option. We must remember that most beings want to satisfy their desires. My beautiful cat Tybalt will always whinge when he sees me entering the kitchen. He knows I am a softy and usually persuades me to give him a little treat. Well, we are not much different from our pets; however, we can learn to be more mindful about differentiating between "need" and "want". We have to develop our mindfulness muscle, which can help us make wise decisions and connect to our ability to be compassionate with "the wild beast" or "the anxious child" within.

Important Facts About Food

The following facts and tips will help you revolutionize your relationship with food.

Awareness of Hunger

We have a belief that we need to eat three meals a day. Of course eating together can be very important for bonding with others. Nevertheless, listen to what your body is telling you. If you are alone, you may decide to have only a very small snack; and if you are sharing a meal, ask yourself before you serve yourself, "How hungry do I feel?" You can always start with a small helping and then have some more. Remember that you can trick your mind by using small plates. Also, a small snack in between meals (such as fruit or nuts) can help you not feel starving and not eat too fast at mealtimes.

Drink Enough Water

Often, we confuse thirst with being hungry. Make sure you drink 2–3l (3½–5pt) of water throughout the day (not immediately before a meal, as it would dilute your digestive juices, but maybe 20 minutes beforehand). Do not drink too much with or directly after eating, so that your digestion can work optimally. Herbal teas count, too.

Being with One Thing Only

You will find it much easier to eat "enough", and to deeply enjoy and savour your food, if you sit at the table, without the distraction of television or computers. Try to eat the first few bites mindfully (tasting, smelling and savouring).

Eat Smart, Eat Fresh

Foods that are fresh, light and colourful can really help to take away the first pangs of hunger and also offer you the vitamins and minerals you need. So start with a salad, carrots or cucumber with hummus or quark, or a vegetable smoothie.

Eat Foods Your Body Really Benefits From

- Bright and colourful fruit and vegetables tend to be the ones rich in minerals and vitamins.
- Wholemeal carbohydrates take more time to be processed by the body, so you tend to stay satisfied for longer and your digestion will work more effectively.
- Unprocessed, unrefined and fresh are best! Ideally from local farmers and food that is in season.
- Protein will fill you up and will tend to help you with weight management (white meat, fish, lentils, beans and so on).
- Use natural cold-pressed oils. You can even get olive-oil sprays, so that you can prepare your meal with less fat.
- Either prepare your own muesli or at least choose a sugar-free variety.
- Some people are very sensitive to modern wheat, which has been genetically modified. Try and choose oats, barley and rice-based varieties of cereals and breads.
- If you like jam, ideally choose one that has been prepared with fruit juice, but even then watch the quantity you eat.

Food Journal

Make sure you keep a food journal for two months, so that you develop a new way of consuming food: a mindful, compassionate way. This offers a wholly different method of thinking about food. Rather than writing down afterwards *what* you ate, you should write down *how* you ate it.

Ask yourself the following questions after breakfast, lunch and dinner and record your answers in your journal.

- Did I eat slowly or quickly?
- Did I eat too much?
- Did I feel too full or just right?
- Was I aware of what I was eating?
- Did I eat a healthy meal?
- Did I feel calm while eating?
- Was I grateful for my food and drink?

Practice: Meditation to Reduce Cravings

We know from research that food cravings are often due to learned behaviour, experiencing stress and having neuropathways in our brains that frequently formed well before we could really understand what responses they triggered. The good news is that cravings rarely last longer than 15 minutes. This meditation is a practice to help you "see and accept" your cravings, recognize them for what they are and not succumb to them too easily. Just give it a try.

Duration: 10–15 minutes

1. Find a comfortable position, either sitting or lying down. Now bring your awareness to your body and the points of contact between yourself and the surface you are resting on. Continue by anchoring yourself, feeling the simple breath of life, coming and going.

2. Now deeply sense your body, seeing whether you can feel where in your body and mind you are feeling your craving and how it presents itself: do you have visions of the food you are craving? Do you feel a pulling, stabbing, heat, emptiness or any other type of discomfort in particular areas of your body? Can you imagine certain smells or tastes, and notice more saliva building up in your mouth? Can you even imagine the texture of the food? Bring a sense of compassion and curiosity to this whole experience.

3. Now try to simply be with these sensations, perhaps saying some words of comfort to yourself: "Soothing, soothing, ease, ease" or any other kind word or phrase that enables you to be with this sense of craving.

4. You may even want to use some compassionate touch: placing one hand on your chest and one on your abdomen – soothing, soothing.

5. After a while I invite you to let your sensations recede into the background of your awareness, and to focus again on breathing in and out, staying with this simple breathing for a while longer.

6. Sooner or later you will probably notice that your sense of craving is lessening. You will start to comprehend that experiencing cravings does not necessarily mean that you have to follow through with an action. Being with and accepting "what is" can be the first step toward a new beginning. If you manage to practise this meditation repeatedly, you may find that cravings for a particular food lessen more and more. You are actively forming a new neuropathway and at the same time reducing your levels of stress, which has multiple advantages.

Mindfulness for Our Planet

"Your food shall be your medicine and your medicine your food."

– Hippocrates, ancient Greek physician, regarded as the "father of medicine"

This text on mindful eating would be incomplete if we did not also consider, as compassionate beings, what consequences our habits of food production and consummation have on other people, and the rest of the world. So let us ponder what it means to eat, harvest and sell food mindfully.

You may be aware that our whole planet is in danger, and so are its inhabitants, due to the exploitation of its natural resources and imbalanced food production. In her book *Harvest for Hope: A Guide to Mindful Eating* the world-renowned primatologist and researcher Jane Goodall writes about how easy it would be for all of us to improve the state of this Earth if we became more aware and compassionate toward all beings.[2]

Many people believe (rightly or wrongly) that less meat and dairy in their diet would improve their wellbeing. A fascinating read is *Peace Food* by the Austrian physician Reudiger Dahlke.[3] He writes about the abominable treatment that animals reared in large quantities experience. You need to be quite tough not only to "digest" reading how we make these animals suffer, but also to consider the cost to our environment and the poorer inhabitants of our planet. We are all interconnected.

From huge areas in the Amazon rainforest we purchase soya, which in turn is used to feed cattle in Europe and Asia. These animals are the cheap meat that we can buy in bulk from many supermarket chains. Neither are the animals fed according to their needs, nor have the indigenous people the opportunity to plant and grow the food they require for their own survival.

Another unbelievable fact is the amount of water you need to invest in order to rear 1kg (2lb) of beef: you need 30,000l (52,800pt) of water. In many areas of the world there is such lack of water that hardly anything grows at all. Can we justify the huge meat production that we invest in?

To find out even more facts, you may wish to watch the movie *Earthlings* directed by Shaun Monson, which has won numerous awards.[4] The sufferings that animals must go through are countless and severe. The way they are handled adds more pain to the whole sad tale of mass meat production. How can we have become so unnecessarily cruel toward other beings? Mahatma Gandhi is said once to have commented, "The greatness of a nation and its moral progress can by judged by the way its animals are treated."

One of the best-known studies discussing the connection between food consumption and health is the China–Cornell–Oxford Project.[5] The lead researcher, T Colin Campbell, points out how overconsumption of animal-based foods can lead to several degenerative diseases and early ageing, due to a large extent to the lack of antioxidants. Therefore more and more people choose to integrate larger proportions of fruit and vegetables into their daily eating plans.

In the end, each of us must decide whether or not to go for organically grown food and free-range products, which tend to taste better, but – due to smaller harvests – cost relatively more. Many indicators point out that organic, and possibly even vegetarian, food will improve overall health and, if eaten correctly, help you stay at a healthy weight. Maybe you can ask yourself mindfully: "Can I really accept cheap products, even though I know they may be responsible for the suffering of the poor, the animal beings and the soil of our world?" Even though it might be impossible to be 100 per cent committed to the pain-free production of nourishment, it may be preferable to be discerning, whenever possible.

On the other hand, we now know that lots of vegan replacement produce, such as vegan cheese and mayonnaise, is made from cashew nuts. These require huge amounts of land to grow on, in order to harvest the vast quantities required for these replacement products. It is the savannah in Brazil, and its unique natural habitat, that is being destroyed to produce the quantity needed by the modern vegan market. I cannot believe this is the ideal alternative! Maybe we need to find the "middle ground" once again, and really focus on locally available goods.

So what can you do to make sure that you are eating well without causing suffering to others?

- Please buy from local farmers.
- When you go shopping, take your reusable shopping bags along and refuse plastic carrier bags (my sons have been calling me a "bag lady" for many years, but I am no longer alone).
- Try and eat produce that is in season, and so has not got to be flown in from distant places (you will reduce your carbon footprint and help small businesses nearby).
- If you must eat meat, choose organic and free-range products.
- How about some mindful gardening: grow some herbs and fruit/vegetables: tomatoes, carrots, strawberries, parsnips, beans and peas, cucumbers, courgettes and pumpkins. Potatoes can be grown in bags just outside your kitchen door.
- Make your own jams and chutneys, and gift others your home-grown foods – what a joy!

Metta Meditation

Metta is a loving-kindness meditation. Loving-kindness is generated through self-compassion – we begin the practice by focusing on ourselves, then extend that compassion to others and then to the whole planet. Use this meditation as explained in the sleep chapter (see page 164), but instead of focusing on sleep, focus on people's wellbeing and on everyone having enough food and water.

Metta meditation includes a declaration. Here is the declaration for the wellbeing of all who inhabit the Earth:

> *May all beings, in the sky, the waters and on land, be safe and protected, may they live peacefully, and may we all share kindness as the greatest common gift!*

> *May all beings have enough food and water to satisfy their daily needs.*

A Morning Prayer – Dear Guardian Angel

Thank you so for watching me
Another day I owe to thee
My dreams were rather wild this night
But Mummy cuddled me quite tight

So all my fears went far away
And I am grateful for this day
For all my toys, my lovely room
My clothes and for my witches' broom!

So sorry that I have to stop
but Mummy's calling, It's eight o'clock
She made my favourite dish again
Porridge, cinnamon and milk in a pan!

I love it so and eat it slowly,
Mindfully, spoon by spoon …
until, my goodness, it's almost noon!

– Patrizia Collard

Mindfulness for Connecting with Sleep

"Sleep health is the most powerful bridge from stress into resilience."

– Natalie Pennicotte-Collier, wellbeing mind coach[1]

World Sleep Day, which occurred on 13 March 2020, highlighted the importance of sleep as a human privilege and a pillar of our health, supporting better decision-making and an understanding of major issues, such as the future of our planet. It emphasized that our general quality of life can be improved by healthy sleep, just as it can decrease when sleep is regularly disturbed.

Sleep is so important because during sleep the body repairs itself. Sometimes all you need is a short rest, so that your anxiety can settle a bit. But often this can be a challenge, and if you are unable to fall asleep, more and more anxious thoughts can start arising in your mind. Globally, insomnia affects 35–50 per cent of the adult population.

It is important to understand the latest sleep research and evidence that even one bad night of sleep – just one – can increase our anxiety by as much as 30 per cent and contribute to raised stress levels within the brain (increased cortisol). This leads to an impairment of our ability to regulate our emotions. People with insomnia have greater levels of depression and anxiety than those who sleep normally; in fact they are ten times as likely to suffer from clinical depression (see page 114) and 17 times as likely to have clinical anxiety.

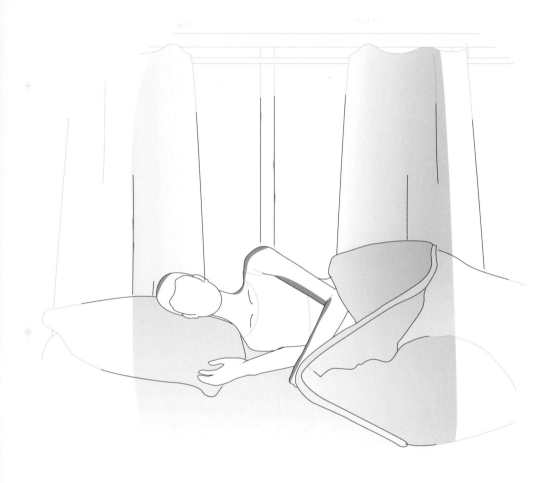

The National Institute of Mental Health's Epidemiologic Catchment Area study found that the risk of developing depression was 39.8 times higher for insomniacs than for those without sleep problems.[2] Other research suggests that too much sleep – particularly too much rapid eye-movement (REM) sleep – can also bring on a depressive state. Too little sleep is around less than six hours, and too much probably more than 12 hours. If you recall the section on depression earlier (see page 114), one common sign of clinical depression is sleep disturbance – early-morning waking, or sleeping for much longer than usual. However, hiding in bed from the world will not restore your mental health.

Furthermore, lack of sleep can impact on our physical health and mental agility. During the normal cycle of sleep we spend about 20 per cent of the time in REM: a unique phase of deep sleep. However, disrupted sleep derails this cycle, causing negative consequences for the memory, the nervous system and the immune system.

During our deep sleep at night the brain is cleansed (almost like a sewage system) and kicks into high gear to wash away toxins. Therefore ensuring there is ample time for you to reach the deep-sleep phase during the night is crucially important in the defence against harmful levels of toxins. Not paying attention to good-quality sleep can mean that more Alzheimer's-related proteins will build up. And the more protein that builds up, the greater your risk of going on to develop dementia in later life. Overall, poor-quality sleep can make you more forgetful even when younger, too.

There is evidence that men who sleep less than five or six hours a night have a reduced level of testosterone, rather like that of a man ten years their senior in biological age. So a consistent lack of quality sleep will age you by almost a decade, in terms of that aspect of virility and wellness. And it is widely recognized that lack of sleep impacts upon the immune system and makes us far more susceptible to common coughs and colds. And research suggests that a short sleep duration enhances our risk of developing numerous forms of cancer, including cancer of the bowel, prostate and breast.[3]

We are also aware that lack of sleep impacts on the cardiovascular system, because it is during deep sleep at night that we receive the body's most powerful form of natural blood-pressure medication – our heart rate drops and, in turn, our blood pressure goes down.

On a more positive note, good and healthy sleep, which means around seven hours or more, doesn't only aid in the cleansing of toxins, but also improves our brain's cognitive function.

Research suggests that sleep-focused mental-health therapies, such as MBCT and CBT therapies, can help in the prevention and treatment of sleep disorders.[4]

Mindfulness Meditation and Sleep

The research quoted below suggests that even a small amount of mindfulness meditation can help calm our hyperactive minds and improve our sleep. Ute Hülsheger, an associate professor of work and organizational psychology at Maastricht University in the Netherlands, was the lead author for this study.[5]

Participants with no formal meditation training were given reading materials that introduced them to the basic tenets of mindfulness – the moment-by-moment awareness of their thoughts, feelings and bodily sensations. They also received instructions and recordings of guided meditations for four specific mindfulness practices:

- A three-minute Mindful Breathing practice (focusing attention on the breath)
- The Body Scan (moving the focus across different areas of the body, see page 196)
- Everyday mindful tasks – mindfully focusing on everyday tasks such as preparing breakfast or taking a shower (see pages 46–77)
- And, crucially, a loving-kindness (Metta) meditation (see page 170), which sends feelings of love and compassion to themselves and others

Over the course of two working weeks the participants were asked to meditate using different combinations of these exercises for ten minutes each day, before and after work, according to a predefined schedule. In addition they completed a series of questions in the morning, at the end of work and at bedtime, to track their sleep quality, the amount of mindfulness at work and their ability to psychologically detach from work-related thoughts after coming home.

The results indicated that over the course of the two-week period, meditators experienced steady improvements in sleep quality, sleep duration and mindfulness.

In fact, sleep is the best free health insurance there is! One thing is an absolute given: for so many people, the real cause of sleep anxiety and insomnia is stress-related. We will focus on more details about the stress response on page 102. Kindly remember, high levels of stress chemicals circling around your system will generally make it very difficult to fall asleep.

Practice: Sleep Meditation

This meditation can help ease your racing mind, reduce feelings of stress and overwhelm and connect you to better sleeping patterns. Perhaps try this technique first and then follow with the Loving-kindness (*Metta*) Meditation (see page 170). You may develop a strong connection to only one meditation, but I recommend that you do both practices to experience the full benefits.

Duration: 15 minutes

1. Find a comfortable position, sitting in an armchair or lying in bed. Make sure the room temperature is just right.

2. Start by welcoming your racing, active mind. Say, "Here you are – welcome", even if it feels uncomfortable and you would prefer this discomfort to disappear. Kindly understand that meditating for sleep can really give you an opportunity to soothe the mind from the worries of the day.

3. You may experience insights during the meditation, which can shed light on the cause of the insomnia you are experiencing. Rather than avoiding these thoughts, sensations and perceptions, try and turn deliberately toward them. When you do this, even if you find yourself caught up in fear around sleep, and the tendency to label yourself a "poor sleeper", accept that this is quite normal. The best way to reduce suffering connected to sleep or fatigue – and, indeed, to promote naturally the best state for experiencing deeper sleep – is to be in this moment, not in the past or the future, but totally connected to the *now*. If you can learn to let go and be, deeper sleep will arise, and you will, with practice, experience sound rest.

4. Give yourself permission to feel whatever you experience, even when you are not as happy with your current sleep situation as you would like to be. You can also apply this practice when you experience wakefulness in the early pre-dawn hours of the day, while still in bed. Trust in your compassion skills and accept tiredness, fatigue and overwhelm in these moments, when you are feeling stuck. Right then you are in fact in the presence of an opportunity. You have the chance to get to know the nature of your mind and befriend yourself, through the soothing *Metta* meditation on the following page.

Practice: Loving-kindness (*Metta*) Meditation

The word *Metta* translates from Sanskrit as a wish for loving kindness, welfare, happiness and good will to all other beings without exception. Traditionally, monks chant a *Metta* for ordinary people. This prayer has been adapted by mindfulness practitioners to expand the heart connection and foster compassion.

Duration: 10–15 minutes

Metta meditation starts with the pure intention that we wish to increase self-compassion from within. We may use the analogy of planting a seed, which we tend through the practice until it grows into a beautiful flower or a tree. Say your list of affirmations aloud as many times as feels comfortable.

- "May I be safe and protected."
- "May I be peaceful."
- "May I live at ease and with kindness."
- "May I rest and sleep with natural, deeper ease."

These words can, of course, be adapted to whatever sits better with you.

It can be helpful to visualize your "emotional" heart in the centre of your chest – an image of yourself as you are now or as you were as a little child, perhaps supported by a loving elder. If visualizing this is difficult for you, then try seeing your name written in the centre of your heart. Week by week you should expand the practice. In week two you can add somebody you love and care for, after having meditated on yourself:

- "May you be safe and protected."
- "May you be peaceful."
- "May you live at ease and with kindness."

In weeks three and four you can then expand the practice to include people you hardly know, those who may have caused you irritation or hurt, and finally:

- "May all beings be safe and protected."
- "May all beings be peaceful."
- "May all beings live at ease and with kindness."

Starting with the mere intention of loving-kindness, experience has shown me that persistence in this practice can wonderfully enrich our lives. If every one of us managed to touch one other person through this practice, the world would indeed be a safer, kinder and more peaceful place to live in.

Relearning to Sleep

A very busy journalist had a problem that presented itself as early-hour wakening (between 2 and 4am). He had experienced this for several years and it had thus become a deeply ingrained habit. He reported that he felt wide awake immediately on wakening and tended to use the "extra time" he gained by this for dealing with work issues. In a way he almost perceived this extra time as a "gift" from the universe, as he really believed he needed it, because it seemed particularly beneficial for polishing off any new story that he had to hand in on that day. So why then did he feel he wanted to change it?

What he shared during therapy were the following areas of dissatisfaction:
- He felt that his afternoon work suffered, as he was losing concentration. He also reported that he could be a little "short" with work colleagues at that time.
- His private life and his relationships at home had really suffered, because all he could do when he got home was have a quick dinner and then go to bed at around 7.30pm (even earlier than his children). He was unable to read his children bedtime stories or attend any evening events at their school, and his intimacy with his partner had fallen by the wayside.
- He had put on some weight, as he tended to feel too tired to engage in any exercise, even at the weekends.

In summary, he concluded that although he tended to get very good results at work, his own health and his relationship with his family had suffered a lot.

We know, from reports about Buddhist monks, that they often sleep less than other people, but spend a lot of time meditating. Obviously the journalist had no intention of becoming a monk or meditating for hours on end. However, he agreed to experiment with meditating for ten minutes at lunchtime at work, and for another 15 minutes immediately after returning home and before dinner.

He soon realized that these two mindful breaks really improved his mood in the afternoon at work, and enabled him to do a little extra preparation on his next day's publication, prior to going home. He also noticed that he was more alert at home, was able to engage more with his kids and started to put them to bed at 8pm. At the weekends he also observed that, as if by magic, he was able to sleep longer, often to a much more reasonable hour, around 8 or 9am. If the family was still asleep, he used those times at the weekend to exercise at home or go for a mindful walk.

He was more fun to be with, and one evening his partner arranged for the kids to stay with friends. She even sat down to meditate with him, and had prepared a lovely dinner. Thereafter she engaged with him in mindful intimacy, which slowly developed and became more regular over time. The journalist realized at this point how much he had missed the company of his wife and his family.

He agreed with his therapist to stay up a little longer, day by day (just 15 minutes per week), which eventually helped him to go to bed around 10pm. The combination of meditating, gentle sleep-time manipulation and spending more time being with the people he loved, over a period of two months, created new behaviour and an overall happier person. By reconnecting to sharing, love and being with his "pack", and by adding a couple of meditations regularly (for he liked routine), he retrained his pattern and his beliefs. He realized that he could do good work in the afternoon and then let it be, where it belonged.

What we see in the above story is that by little changes, plus the implementation of mindfulness practice and compassion toward himself and others, many things were affected, and a much bigger change could be achieved.

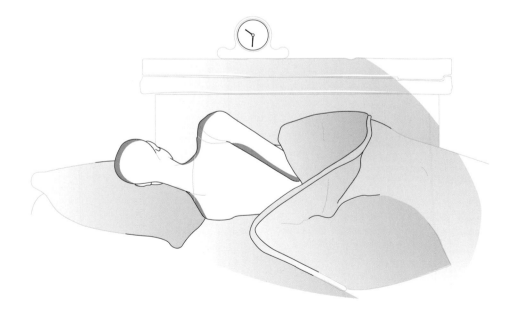

When Sleep Becomes a Challenge

Below are some mindful ways of allowing yourself to let go and get some much-needed rest:

- First, acknowledge that we can positively influence our sleep by *respecting the time for real rest*. This will help the body and mind to unwind through the power of meditation.
- Introduce the sleep ritual of doing an extra-long Body Scan (see page 196), ideally in dim, low-level light or candle-light to enhance sleep duration and quality. But don't fall asleep with a burning candle in the room!
- Write down your three EGS (Enjoyment, Gratitude and Satisfaction, see page 213) in your journal: what you enjoyed today, what you are grateful for and what you are satisfied with.
- Engage your senses away from all screens (the blue light blocks the sleep hormones and has been shown to fragment sleep).
- Switch on some nature sounds or gentle folk or classical music to soothe your mind and switch off from the day.
- Mindfully drink a glass of warm milk and honey or a herbal infusion.
- Have a candlelit mindful hot bath, using aromatherapy oils such as cedar or lavender. There are certain smells, such as pepper, cardamom and other Eastern spices, that increase your sensuality and make you fierier. Other scents, like those of roses or lavender, tend to be more relaxing. Mood-enhancing are aromas like jasmine and sandalwood. So you may wish to experiment a little. Go to an aromatherapy shop or health-food shop and "retrain" your scent awareness. Any oil that you like the scent of, and that relaxes you, is good for you; you need to find your own blend. Then put a few drops into your bath; alternatively, you can dilute your favourite blend in grapeseed oil and put a few drops onto your temples or wrists, or you can vaporize it in an aromatherapy lamp. Here are a few more emotionally uplifting oils: bergamot, camomile, geranium and rosemary. The last two in particular are said to strengthen the adrenal glands, which tend to be on overtime when you are feeling stressed, but they should only ever be used occasionally, I have been told by experts in aromatherapy oils. *Never use these oils long term.* **Caution**: I recommend that you seek advice from an expert who can check which potions are best for you. If you are pregnant, it is always best to check with your healthcare provider first and to seek expert advice.

- As a special treat, you may decide to go for a regular aromatherapy massage. I have a massage therapist who comes to my home. She uses hot stones and aromatic oils. It's very indulgent, but I sleep like an angel afterwards. I always book her to come in the evening after dinner. I can warmly recommend such an arrangement, as deep-tissue massage in addition to the oils really makes you sleepy. Remember: you must rest after this kind of treatment and not drive for an hour or two.

Other Sleep-improvement Opportunities

As well as learning to accept "what is", even though it may be not perfect right now, you can apply other techniques throughout the day to improve your sleep:

- Remember to make best use of morning and daylight hours, and even sunshine, when it is available.
- Take regular breaks to rest from technology. Just breathe, move, journal, dance, sing and so on.
- Exercise, if possible before midday or early afternoon, rather than late in the evening (as this will reactivate your adrenal glands).
- When daylight disappears, our eyes send messages to our brain to switch from producing adrenaline to producing melatonin instead. Therefore we usually feel a little colder at night (less adrenaline), so we may need to wrap up warmer.
- A mindful way of eating that is conducive to helping our sleep pathways is recommended: basically, not too much and not too late – at least four to six hours before going to bed. Vegetables take two hours to digest, white meat four hours and red meat six to eight hours. While our digestion is active, sleep may be difficult to come by.
- Aim to sleep ideally for eight to ten hours. This is a wonderful opportunity to form a friendlier relationship with, and new respect for, sleep; and to enjoy the art of rest.

Peace (A Bedtime Story)

She was like pure light, the little queen! Her hair, bright, like the sun itself,
and her face as sweet as the leaf of a rose!
"I am afraid, I will never ever fall in love with anybody," she once uttered while
strolling along the bank of a lake.
"And why should that be so?" the gentleman, who walked beside her,
asked her caringly.
"I am too quiet", she replied, "I enjoy summertime like a cricket might or maybe like
the swans who live on the lake."
"But there are those who disturb the peace over there on the horizon. What might
they do to us?"
"We may most probably no longer be able to enjoy the summer like the cricket or
the swans on the lake?"
"My dear One, my Sweet…," the gentleman murmured.
"What did you say?!"
"Oh, nothing."
And she continued to enjoy the summer, like the cricket and the swans - - -!

– Peter Altenberg, Austrian writer and poet (1859–1919)[6]

4

THE GIFTS OF LATER LIFE

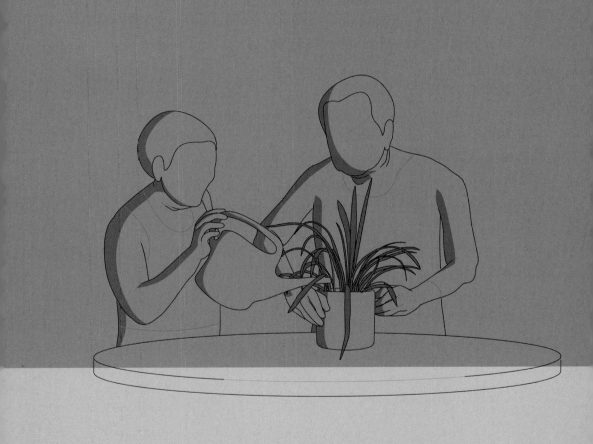

Mindful Ageing:
Grace and Happiness

How can we be in a wise relationship with ageing? There is no simple answer that fits everyone. What I find useful, and will therefore share with you, is simply sitting with "what is" – not trying to change it, wish it away or fast-forward. *Every moment is what it is; every moment passes at last.* Being with "what is" comprises perhaps the most fundamental mindfulness practice of all, and yet the most challenging one for a quick-fix society.

As we get older, we may indeed be wiser for having had more experiences to process and learn from. We may not only need to be slower, but may wish to experience life at a slower pace. One danger is that we look back with a sense of loss for what we thought we wanted to do, but never got round to achieving.

Now that I am in my "second spring" (a term that I coined for women after the menopause, when in many ways they may have more freedom than ever before) I have less thirst for rushing to all the places I have never seen and always wanted to visit. When I sit down in meditation and ponder on why this might be so, I come up with a simple answer. I will never be able to see it all, so maybe it is enough and anything extra is a bonus. I have visited Paris three times, yet never went up the Eiffel Tower. I felt more drawn to sitting in the little cafés, watching people and how they behave – microcosm rather than macrocosm. None of us knows how much lifetime we have left. Therefore it makes sense (for me, at least) to savour each moment: to truly live, right here, right now.

Inspirational Elders

I once attended a retreat held in a large building that also housed a care facility. The theme was "Being with the Difficult". On one of my mindful walks I observed many very old and frail people sitting in a room, either watching television or watching life outside, as if it was no longer happening to them, and I felt deep sadness.

However, I feel very drawn to old people and have met some fantastic ones, and I am always so amazed by the stories they relate. Let me tell you about Charlie, who was 97 years young when he chatted me up on a sightseeing tour in Berlin. He really did make a pass at me – very mindfully, though. I explained to him that I needed to catch up with my group, of which my boyfriend was a part. Although Charlie was a little disappointed about this, he told me he would wait for us both at a Kaffeehaus, when the tour finished. And I am so glad he did.

That afternoon we began a wonderful friendship that lasted for seven years, until Charlie died at 103. Being a genuine Berliner, he showed us the city from a new standpoint, showing us numerous hidden spots known only to locals, and telling us about his life in the silent-movie industry and how he moved to South America during the Second World War and made films there. In his sixties he suffered from prostate cancer and then nursed his bedridden wife, who would otherwise have ended up in a care home, until she passed away. Charlie was completely passionate about life and being alive. He loved going to the airport and mindfully watching people – possibly he was still making movies in his mind.

Here are some other stories about famous people aged 80+ who have lived life to the full, moment by moment:
- The Austrian neurologist Viktor Frankl (1905–1997) survived imprisonment in the Nazi concentration camps and turned down the chance to escape so that he could remain with the inmates who had become his "patients". His "search for meaning" was based on his belief that we all have the freedom to determine our own purpose, and therefore our wellbeing. He later published a book entitled *Man's Search for Meaning* about his own experience as a psychologist of the concentration camps.[1] Frankl also founded the logotherapy school of psychology, and lived in Vienna into his nineties.
- Edith Eger (b. 1928) was a brilliant ballerina when she was sent to Auschwitz and had to dance for the infamous Nazi doctor Joseph Mengele. She stills works as a psychotherapist in the US and published her novels *The Choice* in 2017 and *The Gift* in 2020. The philanthropist Sheryl Sandberg chose *The Choice*

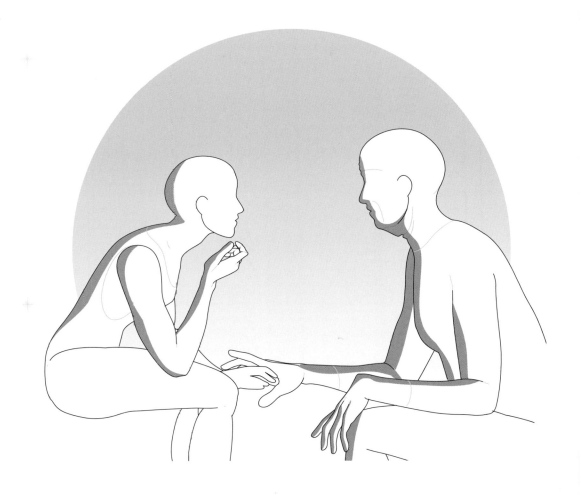

as one of her books of the year, saying, "Her life and work are an incredible example of forgiveness, resilience and generosity."[2]

- Grandma Moses (1860–1961) became a world-renowned naïve painter after she began painting in her late seventies, following the death of her husband. She lived to the age of 101, at which point President John F Kennedy paid tribute to her legacy in helping the nation to renew its pioneer heritage.
- Hans Hass (1919–2013), was an Austrian biologist who invented scuba diving and pioneered underwater photography. He did his last dive at the age of 89, and was known for his innovations in diving technology and his commitment to the environment.
- The author Joanna Macey (b. 1929) is one of the leading experts in climate change, although she only started publishing at the age of 50. She is still active in her nineties.
- And have you ever heard of the famous centenarians of Okinawa, Japan, who live on the "island of long life"? Their longevity is at least partially due to practising prayer and meditation, and to holding each moment as something valuable in their awareness. They simply enjoy being alive.

And so the circle that starts with joy in the adventure of life in childhood closes with that same possibility. There need be no greater purpose in life than this: being alive, now and again now.

Here I wish to mention a man who has inspired generations and has deeply influenced so many people by being an ambassador for peace and reconciliation, as well as a great example of loving kindness and mindfulness. Thich Nhat Hanh had to leave his homeland in order to survive. However, by closing one door, he opened another one and achieved amazing things.

Thich Nhat Hanh travelled to the United States in 1961 to teach comparative religion at Princeton University and Columbia University. In Vietnam in the early 1960s he had started the School of Youth and Social Service, a grassroots relief organization for thousands of volunteers, based on the Buddhist principles of non-violence and compassionate action. He became a close friend of Dr Martin Luther King, who nominated him for Nobel Peace Prize. In 1966 he established the Order of Interbeing and a beautiful retreat centre called Plum Village near Bordeaux in France. He heads a monastic and lay group, teaching mindfulness trainings. More recently he founded Wake Up, a worldwide movement for young people training in the practice of mindful living. In 2014, one month after his 88th birthday and following several months of rapidly declining health, Thich Nhat Hanh suffered

a severe stroke. Although he is now unable to speak and is paralysed on his right side, he has continued to offer the Dharma (Buddhist teachings) and inspiration through his peaceful, calm and courageous life. He is presently finishing another book about compassion for our planet and our resources.

What have all these people in common? They have an innate wish to realize their purpose in life. Not simply staying alive, but really living from moment to moment, savouring any chances that we are offered, seems to make life really worth living for 100 years – or more. In his book *The Doctor and the Soul*, Viktor Frankl writes, "This 'search for meaning' is the most human phenomenon of all, which we do not seem to share with any other being on earth."[3]

The well-known psychology researcher Ellen Langer (b. 1947) has studied mindfulness for the last 50 years or more (she regards it as a state of being). When she conducted an experiment in a nursing home in Connecticut, some of the residents were given a few mindful activities to add to their daily routines: being encouraged to water a house plant, for instance, or to make a cup of tea by themselves. A year and a half later the same group demonstrated increased alertness, raised levels of cheerfulness and higher activity levels compared to the other residents; and fewer of them had died, compared to the control group. This encouraged Langer to start a ten-year project on the effects on ageing of mindfulness versus *mindlessness*. As a Harvard psychology professor who has authored 11 books on successful ageing and decision-making and mindfulness, Langer shares: "Mindfulness (conscious awareness of and focus on the present moment) is important; placebo effects cannot be discounted; and evidence supports the benefits of making sure people maintain agency and independence as they get older."[4]

In a 2017 podcast entitled "Science of Mindlessness and Mindfulness", Langer explains, "Ultimately, I think that for me, what it means to be human is to feel unique, but to recognize that everybody else is also unique. And I think that people – right now, I think people feel that being happy, really happy in this deep way that I'm referring to, not that you've just won an award or bought something new or whatever – that they think that this is something that one should experience sometimes; maybe if you experience it a little more than other people, you're one of the lucky ones – where I think it should be the way you are all the time."[5]

Myself, I certainly look and act a good decade younger than I am, or so people say. When I travelled to Papua New Guinea, indigenous people there never knew their birthday, they talked of children and very old and wise ones; everyone else belonged to the category in the middle, which is, perhaps, a worthwhile way to view ageing.

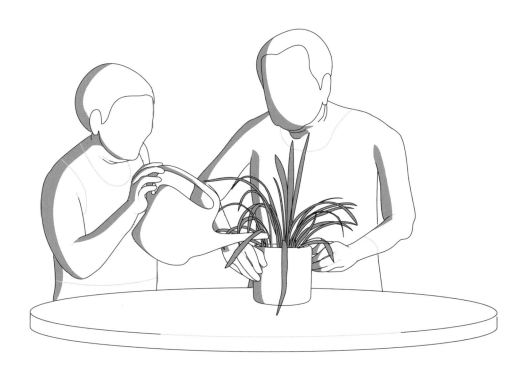

Practice: Viewing Mindfulness

Life is precious and it can be wonderful, but even bitter moments can enhance our understanding of life and our insights. We cannot say how long we will walk this Earth and breathe its air. However, a recent study has shown that mindfulness meditation might extend our lives, as well as being responsible for structural changes in the brain. As reported in *The Observer* in April 2011, "One result has potentially stunning implications: that by protecting caps called telomeres on the ends of our chromosomes, meditation might help to delay the process of ageing." But why would we want to stay alive longer, unless we have the curiosity to learn and experience more, moment by moment?

Here is a practice that invites you to notice a new aspect of life, to which you have previously not paid much attention.

Duration: 10 minutes

1. Spend ten minutes or so really looking at one leaf on a tree, or at a particular flower or stone. Alternatively, if you are inside, you might want to pick up a small piece of furniture or an ornament that you like, wondering how it began life and how many people were involved in creating it.

2. Focus solely on this one object and after a while you may notice how many different aspects of it you begin to be aware of: its shades of colour, shadows, indentations and so on.

3. In time you will notice that your breathing has slowed down, and you may experience a feeling of deep peace within you.

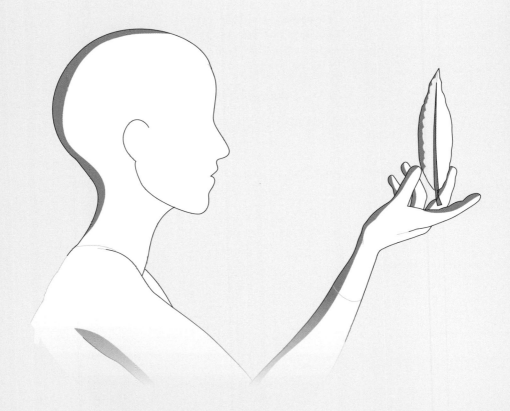

Autumn Day

Lord: it is time. The summer was enormous.
Lay down your shadow on the sundials,
And on the meadows set the winds free.

Command the last fruits to fullness;
Grant them two more southerly days,
Press them toward perfection and chase
The last sweetness into the heavy wine.

– Rainer Maria Rilke, Austrian poet (1875–1926)[6]

Illness and Caregiving

Illness can totally take over your life, whether it is a short-lived and intense illness, a potentially incurable and chronic one or an illness that, when it is healed, requires you to adapt to a totally new way of being alive. Mindfulness teachings encourage us first to accept what is here, even if we really do not want it, and then to respond mindfully to the experience, with wisdom and patience. This may give us the best chance of adapting skilfully to the situation we find ourselves in. Of course this attitude is very hard to apply if you are dealing with long-term illness or the loss of mobility, a limb or your looks, due to an accident or a fire. However, acceptance may help us not merely exist due to our illness, but also learn to live around it, with it and settle into a meaningful life in spite of it, as best as we can. The only thing we know for sure is that everything changes all the time. Even with incurable diseases or the loss of a previously functioning body, change is still possible. What kind of change and how soon: those are the aspects we need to be patient with. We simply do not know, and it is an ongoing journey.

Jon Kabat-Zinn, the revolutionary scientist who created MBSR in the 1980s, first worked with patients suffering from chronic pain and the skin disorder psoriasis. Both conditions significantly reduced in intensity when patients engaged in practising mindfulness. Those with chronic pain, who had become mere observers of other people's lives, started to live their lives again. Those with psoriasis experienced a much faster recovery from their skin condition during treatment, and longer periods without symptoms being present. Kabat-Zinn published numerous research papers about these two client groups. While patients were receiving infrared-light treatment to heal their skin, one group (the control group) was listening to classical or relaxing music, whereas the other group was listening to the Body Scan meditation (see page 196). The latter group improved in half the time – and that is quite something.

So this is a wonderful point to introduce the Body Scan exercise. As with earlier practices, please read through the instructions first, before attempting it.

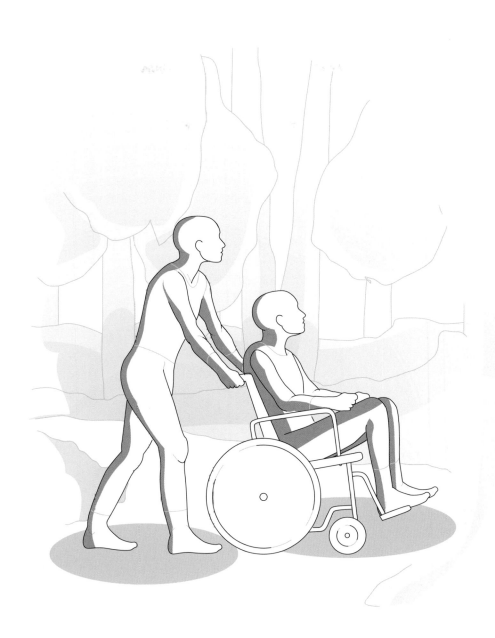

Practice: Body Scan (1)

This exercise is particularly useful for getting in touch with your whole sensory experience. With this practice you gradually travel through your body: the areas you are less aware of, the ones you already know and other parts that may cause problems or pain. By truly opening yourself to this experience – this journey through the "within" – you learn to understand what your body is trying to tell you, and that not every part of it is broken. It can help you to create a healthy relationship with a body that you may deem imperfect. Yet this is the house you live in: this is all you've got. Can you accept it and even feel some gratitude for all the parts that are actually working?

While bringing awareness to each body part really creates a portal into mindfulness, you may at times experience discomfort or even pain in certain areas. Should this be the case, you may find it helpful to remember that you will soon attend to a different area, which usually reduces the intensity of the discomfort you have just felt. Should any intense pain persist and not seem to shift at all, the wisest thing might be to change position.

Duration: 30–40 minutes

1. Make yourself comfortable somewhere you will not be disturbed, in a place where you will be warm, perhaps lying on your back on a mat or rug on the floor, on the sofa or on your bed. Allow your eyes to close gently.

2. Take a few moments to get in touch with the movement of your breathing. When you are ready, bring your awareness to the physical sensations in your body, especially the sensations of touch where your body is in contact with the floor or the bed. On each out-breath allow yourself to let go, sinking a little deeper into the surface beneath you.

3. Remind yourself of the intention of this practice. Its aim is not to feel any different, more relaxed or calm – this may happen or it may not. Instead the intention is, as best you can, to bring awareness to all the sensations you observe as you attend to each part of your body in turn.

4. Now bring your awareness to the physical sensations in your chest and your abdomen, to the changing feelings in the chest and abdominal wall as you breathe in and breathe out. Take a few minutes to feel the sensations as you inhale and exhale. It may be helpful to put one hand on your chest and the other on your belly, and to really feel each breath as it comes in and leaves the

body, noticing that some breaths may be deeper and others shallower, and that there tends to be a little pause between each in- and out-breath. Some may be longer, others shorter ... Each breath is a new experience.

5. After a while you can gently put your hands back into their original position and change your anchor of awareness to your "body as a whole". I shall take you through a journey where sooner or later you will discover yourself anew. Truly inhabiting your body – and not just your brain – may help you get clues about your overall wellbeing, and state of mood and health, in a fresh and immediate way.

6. So having connected with the sensations in your chest and abdomen, bring your focus down the left leg, into the left foot. Focus on each of the toes of the left foot in turn: the big toe, the little toe and the toes in between. Bringing a gentle curiosity even to the spaces between the toes: sensing them or simply knowing that they are there. Perhaps notice a tingling or warmth – or no particular sensation. Whatever you find, that is exactly how it is and therefore okay. Now broaden your field of awareness to the rest of the left foot: the sole, the heel, the upper part, the little bones and blood vessels, the ankle and even the skin covering your foot. Then continuing to move your awareness further up your left leg, to the calf, the shin, the knee and the thigh.

7. All the while there is the possibility of your mind wandering off into daydreaming, planning, remembering ... That is the nature of automatic thought processes: they are going to be present again and again. Do not fight them, but see where the mind has led you and then, without judgement, escort it back to the Body Scan. Imagine calling a little puppy or child that has run off, encouraging it to return. Even if this happens hundreds of times, do not worry. Instead congratulate yourself on having noticed the wandering mind.

8. When you are ready, on an in-breath, feel the breath entering the nostrils, then the lungs and passing down into the abdomen, the left leg and the left foot. Then, on the out-breath, feel or imagine the breath coming all the way back up, out of the foot into the leg, up through the abdomen, chest and out through the nose. On each out-breath feel a release of any tension or discomfort. As best you can, continue this for a few breaths, breathing down into the toes, then back up from them and out through the nose. It may be an unusual thing to do, but with the help of your intention it should become easier and easier practising this "breathing into", approaching it playfully, with the curiosity of a child.

9. Having completed the journey through your left leg in this way, notice how it is feeling now, compared to the right one. Are you aware of any differences in sensation, such as a tingling in one leg and not in the other, heaviness versus lightness and so on? There may or may not be any difference. Whatever your experience is – there is no right or wrong way of doing this practice – gently bring your awareness to it and observe with interest whatever you find.

10. Now mentally let go of your left leg and repeat the same steps on your right leg.

11. After completing the passage through both legs, allow them to recede into the background of your awareness and bring your torso centre-stage. Start by focusing on your sitting bones and buttocks, then the hips and reproductive areas, the belly and belly button, the chest and ribcage, the collarbones and shoulders, the upper, middle and lower back and your spine, vertebra by vertebra, being present in every moment.

12. Now focus on some of your vital organs, starting with the heart, then the lungs, the liver, the stomach and digestive tract, the kidneys and urinary tract. Of course you may add any other body part that seems relevant to you and that might need gentle attention.

13. Having scanned your whole torso in this fashion, gently breathe into it and allow any tension or discomfort to be released on the out-breath. Keep repeating this a few more times. Should you start falling asleep at any point, you may find it helpful to prop your head up on a pillow or to open your eyes a little and continue the practice this way, remembering that the intention of the Body Scan is to fall awake to the experience of being alive in your body. There is no need to feel guilty, though, should sleep envelop you; it may simply mean that you are truly tired and need some sleep. Have a sense of compassion for your whole body during this practice.

14. Now bring awareness to your left arm and hand. Start with the fingertips and then the thumb, index finger, middle finger, ring finger and little finger. Shift your focus now to the palm of your left hand, then the back and the knuckles. Move up to the left wrist, forearm and upper arm.

15. On the next in-breath, breathe into your left arm and hand, releasing any tension or discomfort on the out-breath. After repeating this, breath in and out a couple more times, moving to the right arm and hand, and repeating the practice as you did with the left arm.

16. Now mentally let go of your arms, hands and torso, and shift your focus to your neck and head area. Start with your neck and throat, cheeks and chin, mouth, lips, teeth, tongue and gums. Continue with your ears and earlobes, nose and nostrils, and the eyes: the sockets of your eyes, the eyeballs, eyelashes, eyelids and eyebrows. Move your awareness to your forehead, temples, the back and crown of your head.

17. Imagine breathing in deeply and sending clear, refreshing energy to every cell of your body, releasing any tension or discomfort on the out-breath. Repeat this a few more times and then return for a while to observing your breathing. Just lie there, breathing in and out.

18. Finally start stretching a little, wriggling your toes and fingers, opening your eyes and orienting yourself. After a couple of minutes or so, turn to your left side and then very slowly come into a sitting and then a standing posture.

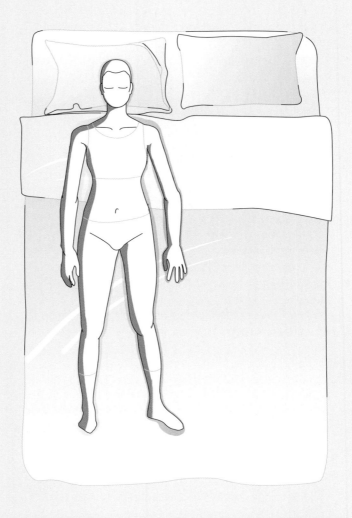

Practice: Upright Body Scan

You may prefer to do this shorter Body Scan in a seated position, with your feet firmly planted on the floor, or stand. Feel free to gently hold onto the back of a chair if you are not sitting.

Duration: 5–10 minutes

1. Place your feet firmly on the floor, hip-distance apart, and straighten your spine. Gently roll your shoulders back and rest your hands on top of one another (if sitting).

2. Take deep cleansing breaths in and out. Stay with your breath until you feel ready to begin.

3. Kindly soften your forehead, your face, your neck. Bring your awareness to your left shoulder, the left elbow, the left wrist, your left hand. If you feel any tension breathe into this part of your body; on each out-breath feel a release of any discomfort.

4. Connect with your left hip, your left knee, then focus on your left ankle. Soften and breathe.

5. Now, focus on your right shoulder, your right elbow, your right wrist. Bring the awareness to your right hand.

6. Take a few minutes to pause, feel the sensations in your body as you inhale and exhale. Each breath is a new experience.

7. Move to your right hip, your right knee, your right ankle. What thoughts are arising right now? There is no need to fight your thoughts. Remember, thoughts are not facts. Allow your thoughts to float away. Bring your mind back to this Body Scan.

8. Inhale deeply, see this breath sending refreshing energy to every cell in your body, releasing any tension or discomfort on the out-breath.

9. Slowly conclude this meditation by feeling the connection points between your feet and the surface they are resting on. Wriggle your toes and fingers, have a big stretch and open your eyes.

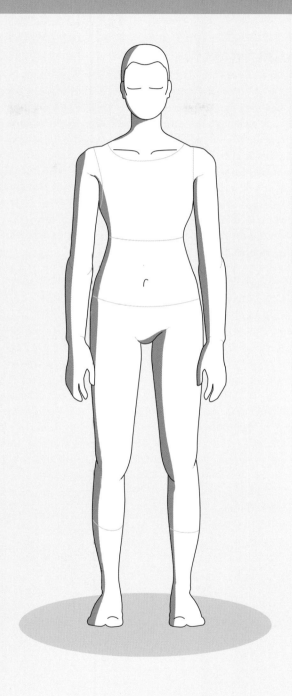

Rebuilding a Life

I want to tell you now about a wonderful therapist I know, who is such an inspiration to me. When she was a teenager she broke her neck in a motorcycle accident and can now only move her hands and feel her body from her chest upward. However, she works as a therapist and meditation teacher and has an enormously purposeful life – her whole attitude of acceptance is a source of great motivation to her clients. She works not only with patients who have suffered spinal injuries, but with anybody who requires her services. She always tells them about her accident and then continues, "So now that is out of the way, kindly tell me why you have decided to start therapy." She has accepted her paralysed body and is so calm about it all. But she always buys ridiculously expensive shoes with high heels, and says, "I don't need to walk in them – they are just for show, and so sexy." To me, she personifies mindfulness and acceptance.

Initially accepting "what is" if you have an illness, and then bit by bit seeing how you can regain some control over your life, rather than letting the diagnosis label you, embodies a mindful approach toward illness. Aaron Beck, the founder of cognitive therapy, demonstrated this idea beautifully in 2005 at a conference entitled "Making Sense of the 21st Century". Beck explained that he had arthritis in his hands, but emphasized that he never called it "my arthritis", but "the arthritis", which helped him feel less overwhelmed by it and less upset about it.

Let me tell you the story of the two arrows, which the Buddha related to his visitors to demonstrate that pain is often a given, but suffering is optional. If life shoots an arrow at us and wounds us, by not accepting it – by worrying about it, saying it's unfair and wondering how long the pain will last – we tend to shoot a second arrow into the open wound and thereby extend and increase the pain. Mindfulness teaches us that each moment is a new beginning and we never know which way the wind will turn.

Difficulty and Delight

The human brain
Can be a pain.
But there's much to learn,
Inner wealth to earn.
Sometimes joy is there with sadness,
Pain igniting playful madness.
Side by side,
The joy and woe,
Given space,
They come and go.
Compassion stronger, Patience longer,
Mountain-like strength,
With fear at arm's length.
Step-by-step
We learn and grow.
With each challenge, somewhere to go.
Mindfulness, a faithful friend
The answer clear, in the end.
A gift to send, a friendly word
Love, compassion, space to feel
Then time allows the pain to heal.

– Dr Karen Neil, inspired by Jo W, who is living courageously with ME[1]

Caregiving During the Physical End of Life

Millions of untrained caregivers spend 50 hours a week or more, over weeks, months and years, caring for a loved one. My own experience was being the second carer of my severely mentally and physically dependent mother – she was cared for by my marvellous brother, but when he was on holiday or needed a break, I took on the responsibility. Mindfulness and compassion helped me to care for her, and helped to reduce her severe anxiety at times. I stayed with her during the last two days and nights of her life, and helped her to pass in her final hours from living into a peaceful death. This was one of my most significant personal experiences of caring.

I used to tell her stories about who was going to be waiting for her and expecting her on the other side, which seemed to really calm her down. I regularly practised the Loving-kindness (*Metta*) Meditation (see page 170) for her, my brother and myself, and frequently applied the Mindful Self-compassion Break (see page 212) as a regular self-support.

Maricel Tabalba is a freelance writer working with a group called Curable Health. In "5 Tools for Mindfulness for Caregivers", she notes that it is estimated that up to 80 per cent of caregivers are not healthcare professionals.[2] Given the physically and emotionally taxing nature of the work, many caregivers suffer from anxiety; and "caregiver stress" is now a medically recognized term. The first recommendation by Maricel is that caregivers should take care of themselves by practising a few minutes of mindfulness on a regular basis. This could include journaling, music therapy, yoga, breathing exercises or Tai Chi, and taking proper breaks every so often. There is evidence that caregivers who look after themselves improve the quality of care for their patient. And do remember to be truly present, when you are caring. The sick person can really feel this and will be deeply grateful for it.

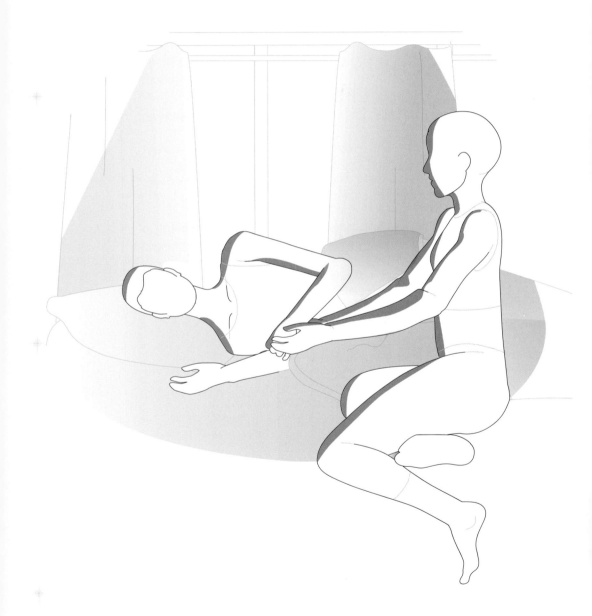

Practice: Connecting with Loss

Loss can take many forms: the loss of a loved one, a cherished animal, the loss of health, of youth, even the loss of a friendship. This practice will help you to sit with the various emotions surrounding any loss.

Duration: 20–25 minutes

1. Sit in a dignified, upright posture in a room where you won't be disturbed. Feel your feet firmly grounded on the floor, your back aligned with your neck and your hands resting in your lap.

2. Start the practice with a gentle focus on your breathing, allowing each in-breath to enter your body and expand for its full duration. Don't force anything, just let your body breathe. Then, after a natural break, exhale on the out-breath for its full duration, until it comes to a natural end. Do this for a while, as long as it takes to feel settled.

3. Now focus on your "loss" (this might be loss of health, a friendship or partnership, or even the death of somebody close to you). Gently say to yourself, "Whatever it is [here you fill in the "loss" either verbally or as an image), let me feel it." So, for example: "My beloved ———, who has left me [or "been called away" – using your own words], I am sitting here and I am prepared to feel the pain of this loss." Start gently with a very simple phrase or image and hold it in your awareness: being with it, feeling and seeing the loss, facing it, even if it is painful, but not pretending it is not there. You may only be able to do this for a minute or two.

4. Then let go of the thought or image and return to the simple breath of life, until you feel the practice has come to its natural conclusion.

The STOP Technique

The Connecting with Loss practice on page 208 is particularly helpful when we are experiencing loss, whereas this STOP technique can help caregivers to take a breathing space.

Joan Griffiths Vega, a practitioner and teacher of MBSR, runs a mindfulness stress-reduction workshop specifically for caregivers at Mount Sinai Hospital in New York. She developed the short, but very effective, STOP practice.

- **S**: Stop what you are doing for a moment.
- **T**: Take a breath. Focus on the in- and out-breath for a few rounds.
- **O**: Observe your thoughts, feelings and physical state. Whatever thoughts there are, let them be or pass. Name your emotions. Notice your body and its posture. Are you hungry or thirsty? Do you feel tense?
- **P**: Proceed with something that may help you now. Maybe call a friend, take a short walk, have a cup of tea and a snack, stretch and let go of tension.

At times you may even have to hire some home help from outside to support you. A single person cannot caregive on their own for very long. Try and avoid "empathy fatigue" and connect to others, even if only by phone or by Skype. When possible, however, let others treat you to tea or even dinner. We need to connect to some wholesome energy when we are caring for the sick. You may even want to join a support group, if time allows and you like sharing your feelings.

Also, try and improve your sleep and really rest deeply, so that you can be more compassionate. And engage in some form of exercise to release endorphins and reduce the stress response. When you improve your sleep, you also increase your capacity for patience.

Practice: Going for a Mindful Walk

Spending time in nature has many benefits: it can improve your mood, boost the immune system, reduce feelings of anger and stress, and promote better physical health. But being in nature doesn't mean you have to drive 30 miles to the countryside — just think "green".

Nature can be any "green" space like a small garden, a park or a forest. In fact, recently, the Japanese practice of forest bathing, Shinrin-yoku, has become popular. Forest bathing involves, as the name suggests, going for a walk in a forest but it is so much more, it is a mindful practice. The main principles of forest bathing are to go in silence and move slowly. As you enjoy Shinrin-yoku, the aim is to walk mindfully, observe the trees and nature while breathing deeply and calmly. You also use your senses to connect with nature: noticing the leaves on the trees, the tiny flowers growing at the side of the path, the bird sitting on the branch above you as the leaves of the trees move gently in the wind.

This exercise guides you in the practice of walking mindfully. The walk can be short, ten minutes, or longer. Please turn off your mobile phone for a little while.

Duration: at least 10 minutes

1. Going for a mindful walk means engaging in walking simply for the sake of it, not to get somewhere. So focus on all your senses.

2. Breathe in the smells of the grass, leaves, wood and sometimes even the rain.

3. Listen to the sounds around you: dogs barking, bicycles passing by, children laughing, the wind, conversations, a plane in the sky.

4. Try and totally immerse yourself in this walk. Feel the ground under your feet: is it soft, hard, moist? Maybe even pick something up – a little pebble perhaps – and feel its shape, its weight, its surface. Then take it with you as a reminder of how beautiful the world seems to your imagination.

And read the chapter Finding Joy and Mindful Activities (see page 220): it is wise to take some breaks from caring and recharge yourself. In this way you will feel better — and that positive energy you will bring back into the caring situation.

Practice: Mindful Self-compassion Break

Caring for a person who is suffering is an intense experience that requires strength and calmness. This little gem of a practice really supported me deeply.

Duration: 5 minutes

1. Start by giving yourself a hug, or stroke your arms, gently hold your own face or place one hand into the other (self-compassion touch).

2. Now say to yourself something like, "This is really difficult. This is a time of suffering" (acknowledging what you are experiencing).

3. Then think: "But I am not alone. Many others are experiencing the same thing right now all over the globe."

4. Fourthly, say to yourself, "May I be safe and protected", "May I be at peace!" or "May I feel ease and safety."

5. Continue by focusing on your breathing for a little while longer, and allow a sigh to arise, should it need to.

Let us now focus a little on what other carers or experts in the field have shared about caregiving.

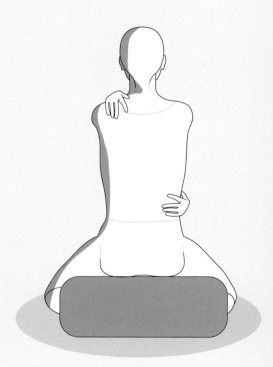

Journaling for Wellbeing (EGS = Enjoyment, Gratitude and Satisfaction)

This practice originated during a research project that Dr Martin Seligman, the founder of Positive Psychology, oversaw. He asked many people to write down three positive thoughts each day. After a month more than 60 per cent of the participants stated that they had noticed a significant improvement in their mood. I developed the idea further, and I ask my clients to write down one thing they *enjoyed* today, something they are *grateful* for and something they did and are *satisfied* with. Satisfaction is less than achievement; it might only mean having mended a tiny tear in a piece of clothing or some other small action that you are personally content with.

Write down your three EGS every day, preferably just before you get ready for bed, which will help you to incline your mind toward something positive before you go to sleep.

Practice: Breathing In for Me, Breathing Out for You

This meditation is based on a practice developed by Chris Germer, a clinical psychologist, and Kristin Neff, who is an associate professor of educational psychology at the University of Texas; together they developed MSC, the Mindful Self-Compassion training programme (see page 29). The benefits of a loving-kindness practice are well documented and include reduced anxiety and depression, kinder self-talk and an increased sense of wellbeing.

Duration: 20 minutes

1. Find a comfortable position on a chair or cushion. Use a shawl or blanket to keep yourself warm, and make sure you will not be disturbed. Close your eyes, if this feels comfortable for you; if not, keep them in soft focus.

2. If you can, put one of your hands on your chest, or anywhere else on your body, to give yourself a sense of being supported with kindness.

3. Start focusing on your breathing. Breathe in and out effortlessly and with ease, noticing how your breath nourishes your body on the in-breath and soothes your body on the out-breath.

4. Now allow your breath to find its own natural rhythm. Be with each in- and out-breath (you may remember this from earlier breathing meditations). If you wish, let yourself feel cradled and looked after by your breathing.

5. Now start focusing on your *in-breath*. Enjoy each breathing in, strengthening your body and increasing vitality. Start receiving wellbeing and compassion with each in-breath. Observe how this sense of kindness slowly spreads through your whole body with each in-breath. It may be that you can perceive more and more self-compassion on each in-breath, and you may visualize compassionate words and images with each movement of the breath.

6. Now start to focus on your *out-breath*. Feel how your body releases tension and relaxes on each out-breath.

7. Remember somebody you care deeply for, or somebody who is struggling with life right now. You know this person could really benefit from your compassion. Allow yourself to manifest this person in your awareness. Now start to focus your out-breath toward this person, gifting them this sense of ease and peace and sending them as much compassion as you possibly can.

8. In for me, out for you.

9. Now let yourself be consumed by the flow of your breathing – breathing in for yourself and breathing out for the other person: one for me, one for you; one for me, one for you!

10. With each in-breath receive kindness and compassion for yourself, and with each out-breath send kindness and compassion to your special person. Find a good balance between breathing in and breathing out; each time you practise it, start afresh – each time is a new experience.

11. Let go of any striving, and allow this practice to unfold naturally. Sooner or later you will probably experience a natural sense of "flow": in for me ... out for you. You might visualize the waves of an ocean coming and going, a never-ending gentle stream ... of compassion ... flowing in and out.

12. When you feel ready, gently bring this meditation to a close. Then rest for a little longer, experiencing the effect of this practice.

The Last Day

And if I knew that this was it
No more to see the sun again
To see you wash your pretty face
And if I knew that this was it
No more to touch your raven hair
Your silky skin and berry lips
To touch with one more kiss
And if I knew
What would I do
My Love, my One my Only
Would hold you tight
And sing for you
The song of songs
The golden lullaby

– Patrizia Collard

5

YOUR ONGOING JOURNEY

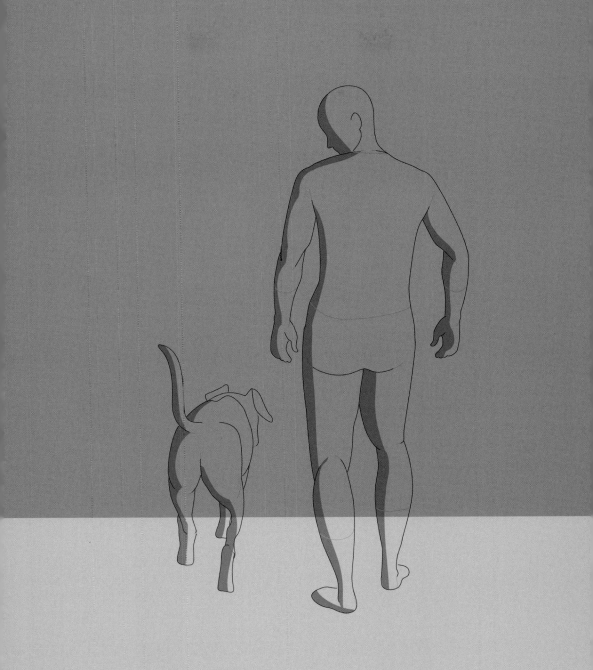

Finding Joy and Mindful Activities

"With our thoughts we make the world!
There is no way to happiness.
Happiness is the way."

– The Buddha

Joy is a small word with a big meaning; The New Collins Concise Dictionary defines it as, "a deep feeling or condition of happiness or contentment". I would like to expand upon this explanation, I believe joy is a state of being that we can discover within ourselves and access through mindfulness practices. When living in the moment, joy can be found in the everyday, the mundane little things, and in this chapter I will guide you through your very own journey into accessing joy. If you are so inclined you can write a Nourishment List, to help you identify the little things that bring you happiness, and furthermore I encourage you to embrace physical activities such as yoga and Tai Chi along with cooking, arts and crafts. Think of this section as exploring and connecting to your inner self. Enjoy!

Mindfulness and Invoking Joy

The thought of finding joy in these difficult times may seem out of touch with all that's happening right now in the world. However, in order to get through any challenging period, we need to stay connected with what is good, uplifting and inspiring us to wish and make a difference.

In times of need, if we can focus on compassion with others and ourselves, and offer little gestures of kindness, good will and understanding, we will be able to ride the wave of uncertainty together and it will pass, sooner or later – of this we can be sure.

The ancient wisdom of Taoism, for example, teaches us that life is made up of 10,000 joys and 10,000 sorrows. If we only focus on the sorrows, we're not seeing the full picture. When we open to joy – the beauty and goodness all around us – it gives us a larger container to hold the suffering that we experience within.

Joy can present itself in different guises: for some people it feels like warm energy radiating from the heart centre; for others, it is a feeling of deep connection with the world and all its creatures. It may be interesting for you to investigate how joy is uniquely expressed through you, and in you, and what the word "joy" means to you.

Write down in your Mindfulness Journal which words or concepts evoke joy in you, how you feel it is most authentically expressed, and any hesitations you may have when contemplating the word itself. If the word "joy" is too "blissful" and does not sit well with you, see if there is another word that resonates better with you. It might be "wellbeing", "contentment", "delight", "happiness" or "aliveness". Once you have found a word that substitutes for "joy", do use it instead, whenever feels appropriate to you.

So what means can we use to focus our awareness on "joy", "delight" or whatever word we use? First, it is important to remember that even deeply content people are not happy all the time. The "10,000 joys and 10,000 sorrows" mentioned above are part of the tapestry of life (with its polar opposites of ying and yang). Let us therefore experiment with our mind (the brain, the heart and the solar plexus) to open to the goodness around and inside us. This may help us become more engaged with life, even in challenging times. It will be important to allow your experience to be whatever it is. Kindly avoid forcing anything.

Another wisdom that has been communicated from Buddhist philosophy is that our mind will become, or will change toward, that which it focuses on most frequently. So mindful awareness can be used to concentrate deliberately on those experiences that we consider positive. What thoughts or actions can lead to opening our hearts and can soothe our minds? Can you come up with a list of acts of kindness and generosity that you either have participated in or heard about? Once again, use your journal. By practising this you create skilful grooves (wholesome thought and action patterns) rather than unpleasant ruts.

Joy is an aspect of life that may seem hidden or dormant right now. However, most innocent babies can experience natural joy. When we're not overwhelmed with stress or suffering, this natural state becomes uncovered and remembered (as often happens during meditation).

In order to increase the experience of joy, you should start by having the intention every morning of being open toward it. Throughout the day we are sowing seeds of one kind or another that will bear fruit one day. "Everything rests on the tip of one's motivation," says a Tibetan wisdom teaching. Intention is different from wishing or hoping. If your intention to stay the same is greater than your intention to change, then you will stay the same. If you have a genuine intention to change, then with practice and patience you will change.

So every morning you might ask yourself, "What is my intention for today?" Visualize what it will look like if you stay connected with this intention and develop more joy in your life some days, some weeks or even a year from now. Is it worth committing to? Get in touch with your heartfelt decision to make this happen to the greatest extent possible. Write down in your journal what proof you would expect to see if your life had turned more toward joy. Would you have met more new friends? Have more people call or invite you round? Would you wake up with a smile most days? What else can you think of?

Rick Hanson, a famous neuropsychologist, has published some fascinating facts on hardwiring the brain for gladness. (He has written numerous books and articles about this, and I have attended many workshops of his, and even invited him as the key speaker to a conference on "Mindfulness and Spirituality" that I organized a while back at the University of East London.) He cites current brain research, which corroborates the power of intention and how we can change. He himself is a long-time meditator and has done extensive research focusing on the intersection of psychology, neurology and Buddhism (see his bimonthly "Wise Brain Bulletin" online[1]) and points out the facts below in his newsletter entitled "7 Facts About the Brain that Incline the Mind to Joy"[2]:

1. The mind and the brain are mainly (and perhaps entirely) a unified system.
2. Neurons that fire together, wire together [that is, frequently thinking and pondering about something inclines the mind in that direction].
3. Fleeting experiences leave lasting traces in the brain.
4. Most changes in the tissues of the brain are in implicit memory.
5. Unfortunately, the brain emphasizes negative experiences.
6. You can help emphasize and store positive experiences through conscious attention.
7. Positive experiences [both those occurring in the moment and stored in implicit memory] have many benefits.

One very helpful practice I have learned is to become deeply aware in my whole body and mind when a wholesome state occurs. Unless we have it on our radar, we can easily miss this. When you feel grateful or happy, or calm or compassionate, it registers more deeply if we are truly present right in the middle of having the experience. (Mindfulness adds to growing this new neuropathway once more.) This is different from vaguely knowing that "I feel good." It's exploring with curiosity the landscape of feeling good.

Practice: Invoking Joy Meditation

Instead of leaving the arising of joy to chance, an important piece in this process is to recognize what evokes it. This exercise is based on *How We Choose to Be Happy* by Rick Foster and Greg Hicks.[3] Once again, use your journal.

In a few minutes, write down a list of everything that triggers the feeling of joy or gladness in you. It can be the simplest thing, like eating a peach, or doing something extraordinary, like diving – or anything in between (stroking a pet, dancing, singing and so on). When you have completed this, check out the points that you already engage in regularly in your life. Then circle other things that it is realistic to include from now on in your life. You will use this list in the meditation below.

It will be helpful to practise this meditation for several days in a row, until finally you only need to visualize the image or the memory, and gladness will immediately permeate your whole being.

Duration: 5–10 minutes

1. Sit down in a comfortable but upright posture. Make sure you won't be disturbed, and that you are warm (perhaps wrap a shawl or blanket around your shoulders). Now reread your list a few times.

2. Then focus on your breathing for a while and close your eyes. Move your awareness toward the area of your heart. If you like, you can put your hand over your heart. If your mind wanders, gently return it to the area of your heart.

3. Now imagine your list like a long, ancient scroll slowly appearing on a big blue screen.

4. Allow yourself to really connect deeply to every single item on the list. Pick one item – perhaps the one that twinkles, or the one that triggered the deepest lasting memory of joy in your awareness. Now, as best as you can, re-experience the situation. Let your awareness register the abundance of joy deeply in your body, breathing in and out this feeling of wellbeing. See whether you can get a smile appearing on your face; maybe you feel lighter and want to sigh or yawn; maybe there are sensations of tingling, warmth and so on in your body.

5. When you have a sense of completion or of "reaching saturation", let the image disappear. Finish the practice with a few rounds of breathing. See whether you can continue breathing in and out from your heart and allow the pure sense of joy to remain there.

Be Mindful of Your Joy

Another regular activity to engage in is to bring your attention straight to your physical and mental experiences while you are in the middle of any wholesome, enjoyable moments: walking in nature, listening to the sounds of nature, watching a sunset, holding your beloved's hand, playing with a child or pet and so on. Make sure that you are "switched on" and "aware" for joyful experiences throughout the day. By writing a "Pleasant-event Diary" regularly (see page 120) you can support this mindful attitude.

Remember that each of us is accountable for how our life unravels. Not completely, of course, but we do have free will (even in a prison cell, as the following story demonstrates) to focus on the beauty of life.

On 17 September 1982 the dissident Russian poet Irina Ratushinskaya was arrested, accused of anti-Soviet agitation for composing and disseminating her collections of verse. She continued writing poems while she was a prisoner in a Soviet labour camp. She wrote using a matchstick on soap, memorizing each piece and then washing it away. She collected about 250 poems during her three and a half years in prison, one year of which was in solitary confinement. Her poems voiced an appreciation of human rights, liberty and the beauty of life. She describes in one such poem, in minute detail, the uniqueness of each snowflake and the deep joy she feels in her heart for being able to notice such beauty, despite her suffering. This is the power of awareness – of noticing loveliness even when one is experiencing despair, separation and fear.

Our relationship to whatever life offers – good, bad or neutral – is what determines how deeply we suffer; or, on the other hand, how we experience joy, despite everything. To comprehend this fact deeply gives you an option: the accountability is yours. You can choose to be glad in the midst of suffering. Both emotions can be present simultaneously.

Ode to Irina

I bow to you
I give you thanks
For your
Awareness
In all the pain
In all the destitute
You still stood strong
And savoured
Like a mountain
The beauty of
Frost-covered
Prison windows

– Patrizia Collard

Create More Joy and Ease in Your Life

Here are some other practices that could help you create more joy and ease in your life:

- Do something nourishing for yourself three or four times a week, or daily if possible (but make no judgements if it is less often): massage, reflexology, Indian head massage, a manicure, pedicure ... Do add some of your own favourites in your journal.

- Engage with your body through movement (walking, running, Tai Chi, Pilates, yoga, swimming and so on) three to five times a week, if possible (for 150 minutes per week, I read recently in a research paper). Watch little kids or animals – they rarely stay still for very long. Doing physical exercise is a way that has proved to many people that their internal chemistry and mood are better at the end than when they started their exercise (more endorphins, once again). I know you've heard it before, but all I'm suggesting here is that you find your own way of exercising from time to time. Remember that we are made of body, mind and spirit. The body contains muscles, and these need to be used or they will wither away.

- You could build exercise into your daily routine by deciding to walk to the supermarket with a backpack (a good one; I don't want you to damage your back) or a new shopping trolley (I have a funky one made of patent leather, with bright tomatoes, lemons and other fruit on it) and then walk home. Or save some money and reduce having a regular cleaner coming in. Housework is excellent exercise, and so is gardening. One of the world's largest studies on physical activity has found that doing household chores can be just as effective as running or working out when it comes to cutting your risk of heart disease and extending your life.[4] So you can bring exercise into your everyday life. It is certainly one of the most stress-relieving activities that research points to.

- Sing or whistle every day, if you can. The shower or bathroom is a brilliant place to practise, particularly if you feel you are out of tune (but who cares, as long as you feel your energy lifting).

- Stay in touch with your intention to incline the mind to more wellbeing. You might spend a few moments at the beginning or end of meditating remembering to identify what brings you joy (see page 220). You could say to yourself, "I want to be open to joy and gladness."

- Remember to observe, with awareness in your mind and body, when you are feeling good, doing something enjoyable, are in the middle of a kind act or are in touch with the blessings in your life – *notice* it, as best you can!

- And, finally, guide yourself from joy to laughter (see page 232).

Laughter

I read recently that a patient suffering from ongoing pain said, "I made the joyous discovery that ten minutes of belly laughter had an anaesthetic effect and would give me at least two hours of pain-free sleep." Now what do you think of that? There is even an unusual therapy called "Laughter Yoga". Dr Madan Kataria, its founder, travels the world holding workshops on how to learn to laugh again. Are you ready to experiment with whether this works for you?

Do watch your favourite funny film or television series (*Fawlty Towers* and *Absolutely Fabulous* still do it for me). Make a deliberate choice to watch funny programmes a few times a week, or you might reread some humorous stories or poems. Maybe sit down with dear friends or loved ones and tell jokes, or remember funny stories that really happened in your life. And when laughter arises naturally, please don't hold it back. Let it out!

Laughing is certainly another exercise that releases your endorphins and increases feelings of wellbeing. Apparently if you laugh a lot at work, it enhances your ability to form a good team that communicates openly and creatively. It even increases productivity. So you might be interested in exploring this avenue.

Laughter is one of the best muscle-relaxants; it expands the blood vessels, allowing more blood to flow to your arms and legs and other muscle groups. And a good bout of laughter certainly reduces levels of stress hormones like cortisol.

Music and Dance

Classical music and certain folk tunes and gentle songs have been recognized as helping to slow down the heart rate, lower blood pressure and switch your state of being to the parasympathetic nervous system. No longer will you produce stress chemicals, but rather you will release endorphins, oxytocin and other wellbeing chemicals. You will feel an improvement in your mood and get a sense of lightness and freedom.

Mindful dancing does not have to be slow; you can put on a tune that really makes you want to let go of any pent-up emotion. For me, Tina Turner still rocks, bless her. "Nutbush City Limits" can really help me "let it all out" and rebalance my equilibrium.

When you engage in mindful music or dance, really be present, letting go of other thoughts and to-do lists. Totally hand yourself over to the flow and be with it, from moment by moment. The biochemist Masaru Emoto wrote in his book *The Hidden Messages in Water* that by using an MRA (Magnetic Resonance Angiography) he was able to measure how music affected the formation of water crystals.[5] Beethoven, Mozart, Bach and the healing tones of "Hado" music (*Hado* is the Japanese word for "resonance wave") created beautiful water crystals at the point of freezing. Using his experimental research on the therapeutic uses of magnetic resonance, Ron Weinstock, a biophysics researcher, theorized that acoustic resonance could have similar healing powers. Not only can music relieve pain, Weinstock believes, but it can actually help strengthen the immune system.[6]

Mindful Art and Craft

Just as with eating mindfully or meditating, we can bring the spirit of mindfulness to creative endeavours, slowing down the actions and focusing deeply on the task. It is important to let go of our perfectionist tendencies and simply engage playfully with whatever activity we choose. The counsellor Bethyn Casey is quoted in the magazine *Happiful* as stating that, apart from improving mood and the feeling of being at ease, crafting may enable us to access and work through difficult emotions.[7] I believe that by allowing our biochemistry to change them into "happy emotions", the brain will indeed be able to access stuck patterns or beliefs and open up to exploring difficulties in a new way.

Here are some crafting ideas, but please feel free to add your own favourite mindful activities:

- **Paper-cutting**: creating elaborate designs, with the use of coloured paper and a craft knife. You could design your own Christmas or birthday cards, or even pictures to frame and give to somebody.
- **Scrapbooking**: should you already have a Mindfulness Journal, you may wish to enhance it by cutting and sticking your own collages into it. You can find material in magazines, or use old postcards or entrance tickets to special places that you have visited. Little memories will literally stick in your book and remind you of the joys in your life, or even show you that life is more meaningful and exciting than you may have thought previously.
- **Stitching by hand**: you might wish to repair a tear mindfully or sew a button back on, or become really creative and use cross-stitch to "paint" a picture in colourful yarns.
- **Woodcarving**: this might be a craft you need to attend a class in, unless you were lucky enough to learn woodcarving at school once upon a time. Making beautiful sculptures out of pieces of wood that you find on a mindful walk through a woodland will truly connect you to nature, and the beauty and peace it can offer.
- **Pottery**: working with clay will deeply connect you to your senses of touch and smell, and eventually to your awareness of colour. You may wish to try some pottery at home or find a local studio that can teach you.

Many of these activities will not only nurture your connection to your senses, but will also offer the opportunity to connect with other human beings, without the use of social media.

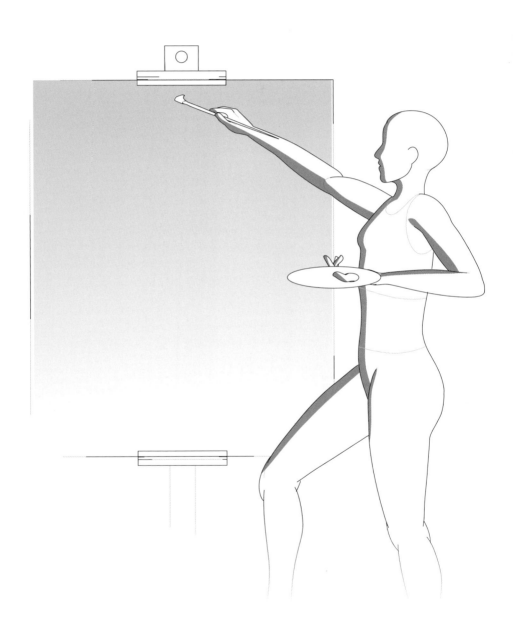

Mindful Dog-walking

Some of you may own a dog, while others may walk dogs as part of their work routine. I have even heard of people who cannot have a dog full-time becoming a "dog auntie/uncle". They can offer a welcome break to the owner, and enjoy a day (or some time) with their visiting doggy friend.

Walking is considered to be one of the best forms of exercise for the body. And walking in nature with a dog in tow will often give you the opportunity to get to know new people that you encounter. Of course it can also be a chore, as dog-walking needs to be done regularly, come rain or shine, but at moments like this you can give yourself a "Mindful Self-compassion Break" (see page 212).

We can learn a lot from our pets, because animals live in the present moment all the time. Dogs use all their senses to explore their walk and, unless they are unwell, they so appreciate every single walk that is offered to them. They have the great advantage of not being addicted to social media, although of course many of their owners are. Alas, research shows that fewer than half of all dog-walkers seem to use their outings as an opportunity to connect more deeply with their pet (and with nature) and to refrain from constantly checking their smartphone.[8]

So, following our dogs' example, let us use all our senses to take in the good, the beautiful, the exceptional, but also the drab – all that a particular walk can offer us. Try and avoid rushing. See whether you can observe the activities of other animals, plus unusual presentations of nature's will to survive (little plants growing out of cracks, for example).

After a mindful walk you will most likely feel refreshed and in a calm mood, and will maybe even experience a stronger sense of belonging (to your dog, to other humans and to nature). Creating this stronger, and possibly more intuitive, bond will also help you notice whether your pet is well or might show signs of any illness or other problems.

You may even at times practise a walking "Body Scan" (see page 196). Appreciate feeling your own physical reality. Scan the different parts of your body in movement. Should you feel tension anywhere, deliberately stop and breathe into this area a few times, releasing on the out-breath. See whether you can add a little playfulness to your walk: just follow your dog's example.

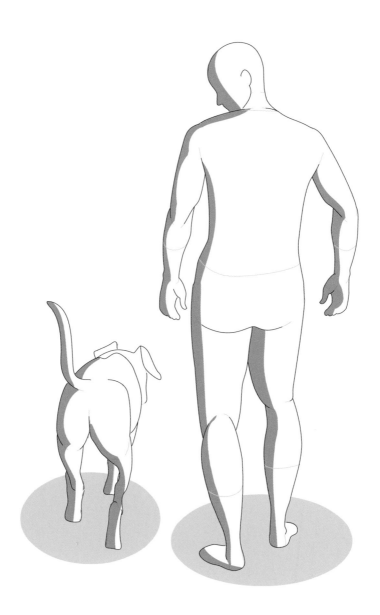

Mindful Cooking

Before preparing a meal, you could mindfully check your fridge or larder for ingredients that you already have to hand, or choose one of your favourite recipes and mindfully write down what you need to purchase.

From preparing to cooking a dish, the whole experience can form an everyday meditation. Should you need to go shopping, for example, mindfully walk around the store and observe the wealth of beauty, flavours, colours and shapes that you can see around you. Once you have selected the produce and washed it mindfully, all actions that are now required – chopping, slicing, whipping, marinating and mixing – will offer you the opportunity to engage with your senses. You may even notice that your mouth begins to water and your appetite increases. Simultaneously being fully present can be an opportunity to find peace and tranquillity in an ordinary task that you might often take for granted, or even resent at times.

Mindful cooking gives us the opportunity to reconnect to a daily activity in a new way. Not only will we be so much more aware of all the different steps that preparation requires, but we may find a sense of gratitude for having the use of our senses and the blessing of such a rich variety of food to choose from. We may even find that cooking a wholesome meal is an act of self-compassion, and often even an act of kindness and generosity when we invite others to share our mindfully prepared meal.

I once participated in a mindful cooking day. We started with a Body Scan (see page 196), then a mindful walk to the local market. We were all invited to choose the ingredient we found most enticing, then returned to the kitchen and, as if by magic, created a wonderful vegetable hotpot and fruit salad with locally grown produce. We were invited to mindfully lay the table, mindfully eat and chew, then continued by washing and tidying up with awareness and a gratitude meditation to finish off the six-hour workshop. I felt nourished in body, mind and soul and met some wonderful folk with whom I am still in touch.

Practice: Self-compassion Writing

Probably most of us feel unhappy about some of our looks, our abilities or aptitudes. Of course we know rationally that nobody is perfect, but why couldn't I be slimmer, have a better-paid job or more caring friends? Here is the opportunity to be "irrational" and really get your frustrations off your chest. Either use your journal or write a letter to yourself.

Duration: 20 minutes

1. Write down everything you feel, sense or think about your shoe size, or your failed driving test, for instance – or some other aspect of your life that disappoints you. This writing is for your eyes only. Let all your emotions come to surface, and if you feel the need to use strong language or vent your anger, feel free!

2. Now, as best as you can, visualize a close friend or anybody who truly cares for you; if you find visualizing difficult, see their name written in your "heart". How would this person respond if you told them what you just wrote, felt and thought about yourself? Imagine this friend loving you unconditionally; seeing you as you truly are – warts and all. How might they respond, in words and deeds? Try to be real, though; this friend truly knows you and would tell you if they thought you engaged in harmful actions. Your wide feet, let's say, are not your fault, but are rather a genetic predisposition. Your impatience may equally be down to genetics, experiences or upbringing, and at least partially not due to your impossible behaviour.

3. Write a response to yourself from your friend's perspective (in your journal or on a nice card – present yourself with a gift of beauty). Think of everything your friend might mention, holding you compassionately in kindly awareness, acceptance, warmth and a genuine intention to help you; and, finally, loving you for who you are.

4. Read and reread the response from "your compassionate friend", who is really your compassionate self! What words or phrases come to mind? Feel your heart respond to their kindness. What do you feel in your chest, your mind and your body?

5. Write down, so that you won't forget it, the power of feeling accepted and loved.

Comfort Zones and Rituals

Comfort zones and rituals refer to places and areas and things we do in them that give us a general sense of wellbeing. The interesting thing I've noticed in my work as a mindfulness teacher is that people often give up those very comfort zones and rituals that would help them keep their head above water, when they are going through periods of stress. The reason for this is generally to save time. They give up the very things that have helped them stay balanced. So be aware of this and always ask yourself, if you notice that you haven't done a certain soothing activity in a while, whether you might need to reintroduce it.

Try and compile a list of comfort zones and rituals: remembering old ones and experimenting with new ones. Use your journal once again to do this. By creating comfort zones and rituals you will actually increase the production of chemicals that de-stress your body and enhance its immune efficiency – the chemicals known as endorphins. The word "endorphin" is short for "endogenous morphine", an opiate that the body can produce itself. No side-effects, no addiction! Self-produced happiness hormones! Endorphins are produced when you feel at peace, at ease and safe.

Comfort zones are places where you feel relaxed and safe and you can forget about all your stressors. They might be a room or even a certain place in your home, like your favourite chair or cushion. They might be a park, a garden, the beach, your favourite pub or coffee house. Rituals, on the other hand, are habits: things you do regularly that increase your feeling of wellbeing. For some people it might be walking the dog or stroking the cat. For other people it's the first cup of tea in the morning. It might be a regular meal out on Fridays – "Thank God it's Friday!" It might be reading a book or poetry or listening to your favourite music. It might be going to the cinema or the theatre. Or talking to friends or meeting them.

Often, of course, our comfort zones and rituals are combined – they are linked together. Like drinking your first cup of tea in your favourite armchair, looking out into the garden and watching the squirrels jumping about, listening to the sound of nature. Remember what I told you earlier about those feel-good chemicals: it is in your power.

Practice: Mindful Yoga

This practice can be done whenever you feel your body is yearning for movement. Ideally your body needs some movement regularly (10–20 minutes a day). Mindful yoga can be done while sitting down, attending to your body.

As with earlier practices, I kindly recommend you read this section a couple of times before practising. If possible, record yourself reading the exercise aloud (using your mobile phone) and then listen to the instructions while letting the practice unfold. Take your time and find peace in movement.

Duration: 20 minutes

1. Start by sitting down, allowing your sitting bones to rest on a chair. Align your spine and neck with dignity, without leaning back, allowing your neck to gently stretch forward by simply moving your chin closer toward your chest. This is your space: here you are!

2. Focus on your feet: remove your shoes, if this feel comfortable, and feel your feet gently resting on the floor or carpet. Can you feel the temperature of the floor – does it feel cool or warm? Rest your hands in your lap or on your thighs. Allow your eyes to shut, if you wish.

3. Gently stretch your toes upward and place them down again. Now stretch the two big toes up and down, then the rest of your toes, up and down. What can you feel in your feet, after having moved your toes in this way? Now press the toes and heels into the floor a little and release, repeating this a few times. Do your feet feel more activated now? Is there any tingling or other sensation?

4. Focus on your thighs: when you try to press your heels into the floor once again, with your hands lovingly resting on your thighs, can you feel your thigh muscles tightening? And when you soften the pressure of the heels, can you feel the thighs releasing?

5. Focus on your knees: gently move your hands forward and let them rest on your knees. Your upper body will move a little forward, too. Can you feel warmth radiating down from the palms of your hands and up from the knees, and a sense of those two energies meeting each other? Now bring yourself back into an upright position, with the hands resting softly on your thighs. Are you more aware of the sitting bones attempting to connect deeply with the chair?

6. Focus on your sitting bones and belly: notice any change in your sitting bones, and allow your belly to be released freely, just like the belly of a smiling Buddha. Continue to do this, moving the palms of your hands forward and backward along your thighs toward the knees. Observe any

pressure in your hands and any change in temperature on the palms of your hands, as you move them forward and backward with ease. Let this movement stop.

7. Focus on moving your upper chest area: move very gently forward and backward a few times and to each side a few times, with minimal movements, seeing what this triggers in your body. Where exactly do you feel the movement? Does this bring a sense of comfort, ease or even playfulness?

8. Now begin to circle your sitting bones gently with tiny rotations, and imagine your whole body and head are held upright by a very thin but strong string. As if you were being moved by a puppeteer, continue this circling, avoiding getting dizzy. You may wish to start circling in the opposite direction. You may feel deeply whatever you are experiencing, due to this movement in your body and your emotions, and possibly observe which thoughts occur while you are doing this. There is no right or wrong way of doing it, but only your way – your body doing this. Make tiny or slightly bigger movements, feeling deeply whatever you need right now.

9. A moment of stillness: after having brought these movements to an end, sit with dignity and complete six rounds of breathing in and out with awareness. Be curious about how your body feels right now, after these gentle rotations. You may notice that your chest area feels more open and released right now. Feel the whole length of your back, from the sitting bones up your spine, vertebra by vertebra, right up to your neck.

10. Now gently rock your whole shoulder girdle to the left and right, including your shoulder blades in this movement – very carefully, as if you were handling a little baby or a pet. Then move your shoulders up and down. Release your arms before doing this and let them dangle at your sides, or place your hands gently on your thighs. Are you noticing your head joining in this rocking?

11. Now invite your whole face to release any tension, softening and soothing all the muscles in your face. You may wish to playfully scrunch up your face and then release all the muscles very slowly again, allowing a soft smile to arise.

12. You may like to imagine your face having the texture of chocolate ice cream, melting slowly in the sunshine: Soften/Soothe/Allow (see page 140). Count from five down to one and really enjoy this soft, broad face as best as you can.

13. Finally, just sit, breathing moment by moment and congratulate yourself for having spent this mindful time with yourself. *Namaste*!

Practice: Yoga to Find Your Centre

This practice for the face, neck and shoulders is particularly useful for relaxing the vagus nerve, which travels from your brainstem, winding down through your body, to finish in your abdomen. On the way it connects with many major organs, including the heart and lungs.

The parasympathetic nervous system is responsible for the so-called "rest and digest" functions and, when we meditate, we encourage our body to switch operational control from the "fight or flight" system to the "rest and digest" system. For centuries meditational practitioners have spoken of "finding your centre" – that area of calm inside yourself where you can gather and control your sense of self. Scientists believe they have found this centre in the vagus nerve.

Only attempt this exercise sitting on the floor if you are very flexible. Otherwise, please choose one of the alternatives on page 248.

Duration: at least 20 minutes

1. Sit upright on a blanket on the floor with your feet hip-with apart. The toes should be positioned straight ahead, as far as this is possible. Allow your knees to be soft and mobile, maybe a little bent, to make sure that your back can be straight rather than hollow.

2. Align your pelvis and your sitting bones so that they seem to be pointing down toward the floor. Now gently allow your belly to become round and soft beneath the navel area, so that it can expand, without creating a hollow back. Aim to be upright with the whole torso. Your spine will slowly seem to lengthen with each in- and out-breath.

3. *Here I am: sitting with dignity.* Allow your whole chest area to expand. Broaden your shoulders, rather than letting them roll forward. Let your shoulders move further and further away from your ears and allow them to hang softly down.

4. Now get a sense of balancing your head on your neck, as if it was the crown of a queen. Gently relax all your facial muscles and allow a smile to appear. Your face should become soft, while widening. Move your chin toward your chest, without changing the position of your head (no looking down). This way your neck lengthens a little.

5. Attempt to feel the point right in the middle of your crown, imagining you are able to grow taller and slowly reaching higher up toward the ceiling.

6. Allow the focus of your eyes to be soft and unfocused. Gently let your arms dangle on each side. Feel your balance in this state of "non-moving". Now see whether you can sense this external balance *internally* too. This will stabilize you psychologically and emotionally. See whether you can exude a sense of self-respect and self-reliance.

7. Now I invite you to gently move your arms and build a cup by interlinking your fingers. It should feel completely easy, without any striving. Now place this cup behind the back of your head and imagine you are cradling a baby's head. So soft, so gentle! Do this with true awareness. Your neck is really long while you are doing it and your arms are gently bent, with your elbows pointing forward.

8. Now breathe out and, on the next in-breath, open your arms sideways, widening the distance between them and allowing your head to rest in your cup, as if it is resting in a hammock. You are now looking slightly forward, toward the ceiling. Your shoulder blades are at the back of your torso, and you can feel a strong deliberate tension between them, which you can actually enjoy!

9. Now, on the out-breath, gently return your head to the starting posture.

10. You are once again looking straight ahead. Your arms have moved closer together again, the elbows are pointing either forward or slightly sideways once more – whatever feels best for your shoulders right now.

11. Engage in this movement eight to ten times, allowing the breath to guide you, relaxing your shoulders more and more and feeling the weight of your head being held lovingly in your cupped hands.

Alternative 1: Not only can you experiment with doing this practice at work, sitting at your desk, but you can even try it out while lying down. The only difference is that while you are lying down, your head is actually resting in your "hand-cup" directly on the surface you are lying on. Your view will now be the ceiling above you. Always endeavour to make the neck loose and long. Focus on your eyes – let them first look up toward your forehead, where your hair starts growing, and then allow them to move down and gently around, gliding in their natural moisture. You can even look gently to the right and the left. Finally look back toward the ceiling.

Alternative 2: Mainly for deep relaxation, allow your head to rest completely motionless in your cupped hands. Your legs can be stretched out on the surface you are resting on, or with your feet standing flat on the floor, knees pointing toward the ceiling. First look upward, then you are invited to move your eyes toward the right and remain in this position for eight in- and out-breaths; the eyes should remain open, but feel free to blink, should this be required. The muscles connected to your eyes are totally soft and at ease. Should you feel the desire to yawn, swallow or sigh, please follow this desire – it is a sign that your autonomic nervous system is getting more and more relaxed. After those eight rounds of breathing in … and out, return your eyes to centre focus, looking straight at the ceiling. Breathing in deeply now, on the next out-breath look with your eyes toward the left. Keep your eyes open, blinking if this feels comfortable. You may once again experience a slight yawning or sighing, allowing any sound of release to occur naturally. Once again, stay in this position for eight rounds of breathing, accepting whatever happens naturally and feeling free simply to be. Eventually return to the middle point, looking directly above you, and allow your breathing to unfold naturally.

Feel deeply into your body, noticing any desire to move a little: this could be more yawning and stretching or sighing. Maybe you want to rotate your hands and feet a little. Do whatever your body is inclined to do at this moment. Then slowly turn your body toward the left or right side, choosing whatever feels best for you and, having arrived there, slowly start raising your torso and begin to sit up. Bringing the session to an end. *Namaste!*

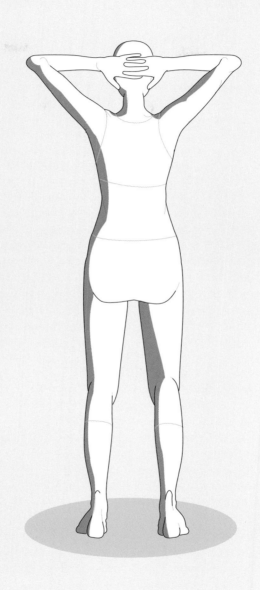

A Mindfulness Journey, Week by Week

Deepening your journey into mindfulness can be experienced in different ways: in a group setting face-to-face with a teacher (maybe even online), using apps or as a self-practice. For the final chapter of this book, I've devised a six-week course for you to follow. Hopefully, after reading the previous chapters you feel confident enough to engage further with your mindfulness journey as a solo traveller.

This course builds on the techniques that you have already experienced; some of the exercises you will be practising are new while others will be familiar from this book but have been adapted to help you build on your existing knowledge, to further strengthen the neural pathways of mindfulness that you have been creating in your brain. This six-week course can be viewed as more advanced, as you are engaging every day with the exercises for a prolonged period, and it will help you to solidify the foundation of your practice. The six modules aim to enhance your awareness so that you can engage and respond to situations (and feelings) in a mindful way rather than using an automatic response, which is often stress-related.

Here is an outline of the course:
- Week One: The Body Scan (see page 252)
- Week Two: The Mindful Minute (see page 256)
- Week Three: Mindful Breathing and Sitting with Your Thoughts (see page 260)
- Week Four: Mindful Movement (see page 266)
- Week Five: The Three-step Breathing Space (see page 272)
- Week Six: A Day of Living Mindfully (see page 276)

I would recommended working through the six weeks in the order that they appear – meaning don't jump immediately to week four or week six! Even if you have prior knowledge of mindfulness, or meditation, it can be helpful to go back to basics to re-engage with your learning.

I would also warmly recommend embracing the whole course and practising daily – even if you only have time for a five-minute session. Don't forget, you can find mindfulness throughout your entire day (see page 46), and we will revisit this fabulous idea, applying mindfulness throughout a longer period, in week six.

Facing Challenges to Practice

Most of us start off enthusiastically when we embark on any new course, but it can be easy to lose your momentum for many reasons. If you find yourself facing challenges, blocking you from engaging with your daily sessions, you may find it helpful to re-read the earlier section on "hindrances" (see page 40).

Where you practise is your choice; try to choose the same spot and make it a comfortable and peaceful experience. Find a restful position (sitting or lying on a yoga mat, comfy sofa or the floor), turn off your phone and perhaps light a candle. This is your precious time to connect with yourself, you deserve this space to slow down.

How to Approach the Six-week Course

If you find any weeks particularly challenging, perhaps spend another few days on those exercises. You may find it insightful to note down your feelings in your Mindfulness Journal (see page 12), too; I have given guidance at the end of each week for questions you may wish to ask yourself daily.

Find the perfect time for you to practise; if you are a lark it may be the morning, if you are a night owl, the evening, or maybe it is somewhere in between. I have kept all of the exercises under 15 minutes to encourage you to fit your meditations into the beginning of your day. Remember, there is no right or wrong way to do mindfulness, just start on your journey and keep moving forward.

I hope that you enjoy this course and discover the long-lasting benefits of living in the present moment.

Week One: The Body Scan

The Body Scan creates a connection between the mind and the body. It is one of the essential practices of mindfulness and therefore it is being taught as the first practice in your six-week course. This meditation is important because it helps you to experience "inhabiting your body" and brings you directly to the present moment.

In addition, the practice introduces compassion and warmth toward yourself, your mind and your body. Throughout the exercise you will be deliberately engaging and disengaging your attention by focusing on different parts of your body. Learning deliberately to shift your awareness in this way gives you greater insight of where your attention is directed and trains the "muscle of shifting attention" to an alternative focus. This ongoing experience of focusing, letting go and refocusing will form new neuropathways in your brain, which will sooner or later lead you to new ways of thinking and being. Little seeds will have been planted earlier during your journey, as you worked through techniques in this book – now these seeds will grow each time you engage with this Body Scan.

The repeated practice of noticing, acknowledging and returning to the body is also in itself an important lesson. We notice that we do not have to attend to our distractions (list-making, daydreaming or worrying), react to them or analyse them. Like sounds around us, thoughts will come and go.

Each time the mind wanders off, we kindly and gently escort it back to the task at hand: scanning another part of the body. We let go of judging ourselves and are reminded to bring our mind to this meditation. We learn that there are no goals to be achieved, no right way for the body to feel. The body is a place to become aware of our emotions, too; it is where we can become mindful of the pleasant, unpleasant or neutral.

The Benefits of the Body Scan

- Connects us to the present moment through our body
- Helps us to understand and accept our body – the healthy parts, the painful parts and everything in between
- Acknowledges and works with the wandering mind
- Encourages us to let go of any self-judgment and "just be"
- Teaches us there is no perfect way for our body to feel

Challenges for This Week

You may find the exercise slightly challenging at first, but please persevere. If your mind wanders during the Body Scan simply view your thoughts as passing events; acknowledge them then gently coax your mind – your awareness – back to your Body Scan.

Try to foster the view that each moment is "as it should be". Don't try to fight or ignore particular thoughts, feelings or bodily sensations – they will only lead you away from your destination. See these thoughts, feelings or sensations as part of your journey.

It can be helpful to approach this week with an open mind and with no expectations. Let go of particular outcomes, experience the experience regardless of what happens with no preconceived ideas of what should happen and how you should feel during or after your sessions.

This week is not a test to be passed or failed, just engaging with the stillness within will benefit you mentally and physically.

Week One Practice: Body Scan (2)

You may prefer to lie on your bed to do this Body Scan, sit with your feet firmly planted on the floor or stand. I suggest recording yourself reading the instructions aloud and playing them back during your daily meditation; this will help you to focus fully on the practice.

Duration: 10–15 minutes

1. If sitting, place your feet firmly on the floor, hip-width apart, and straighten your spine. Gently roll your shoulders back to open your heart space and rest your hands one on top of the other. If lying, let your body sink into your bed or your yoga mat. Feel the connection of your head, your hips and your heels with the ground/mattress. Kindly cover yourself with a shawl or blanket to keep yourself warm because your body temperature may drop during the meditation.

2. Take a few minutes to get in touch with the simple breath of life as it unfolds, without changing it in any way. Just notice the in-breath and the out-breath for a few rounds.

3. Connecting your feet, heels, buttocks, hips and shoulders to whatever surface you are lying on. Really notice this connection, as best as you can, grounding yourself.

4. Now bring your awareness to both your feet and each of your toes in turn. Notice what you can actually feel and then expand this experience to both feet as a whole.

5. Embrace the awareness further up both legs until you have scanned them both completely. Should your mind wander, as minds will tend to do, gently and kindly escort it back to the task at hand, simply scanning your body. If this happens multiple times, so be it; that is the nature of the mind.

6. Once you have a sense of both legs in their entirety, kindly breath in deeply and allow the breath to travel all the way down into your toes. On the out-breath, imagine letting go of any discomfort or tension that may reside in your legs. Do this a few more times.

7. Focus the spotlight of your awareness on your torso, arms and hands, maybe starting with your hips and pelvis, then your abdomen, navel, upper torso, shoulders, arms, hands, fingers, lower back and upper back. Work your way up your spine, as if you were ascending a staircase, until you reach your neck.

8. If you feel sleepy at any time, kindly open your eyes a little. This practice is intended to help you fall awake to your body and the sensations you can find within. However, whatever happens, never be critical of the wandering mind or feelings of sleepiness; compassion rules.

9. Focus on your neck, mouth, cheeks, ears, nose, eyes, forehead, back of the head and crown of the head.

10. Breath in deeply a few more times, sending the breath to every cell of your body, re-energizing your body and letting go of any residual tension.

11. Finally, just sit or lie still, appreciating your body, which has served you so well, for so long, and perhaps even feel a sense of gratitude arise. Before getting up, stretch a little, move your fingers and toes and then open your eyes completely.

What to Write in Your Mindfulness Journal

Reflect on your Body Scan sessions immediately after you have experienced them. While things are still fresh in your mind, ask yourself the following questions:

- Were you aware of any emotions in your body during this practice?
- If so, what type of sensations did you feel and where were they in your body?
- Did the sensations surprise you? What was your reaction?
- Did anything trigger real enthusiasm during the session/practice?
- What was particularly challenging during your session?
- Do these challenges continue to be the same or change each time you return to this practice?

Closing Thoughts

At the end of this first week, you will discover that every Body Scan has different aspects of experience and that all of them sooner or later disappear. Nothing lasts for ever. Everything is impermanent!

Week Two: The Mindful Minute

During the first week of this course, you created a strong connection between your mind and body. In this second week, you are going to strengthen the link between your mind and the breath.

The Mindful Minute is a simple 60-second breath practice where your attention is directed wholly toward your breathing. The breath will bring you quickly to the here and now; it acts as a focus and takes you out of your head and away from racing thoughts, which are often negative. Engaging with this exercise will help you to feel more relaxed when you move onto the longer breathing practice in week three.

The Benefits of the Mindful Minute

- Grounds us in the present moment
- Engages us with the breath as a tool for focus
- Creates moments of calm throughout a busy day
- Allows things to be as they are
- Fosters non-judgemental awareness

Challenges For This Week

Often during this exercise people notice different qualities to their breathing. Sometimes it can feel as if their breath is reacting to their attention and becomes artificial when they pay attention to it! This experience is common, and it is important to relax and try to let the breath be (with no judgement). If the feeling of discomfort is continuous, step back and observe your experience with ease and compassion, exploring it a little. Then on an in-breath, start again breathing in and out, allowing the rhythm of breath to unfold naturally; accept that each breath may be a little different from the one before.

The breath can also become very soft; at times you might hardly feel it at all. If this is the case, try to let your awareness match the softness of your breath. This practice aims to refine your breath attention, to focus on the breath itself and not your response to it.

Week Two Practice: Mindful Minute

This short practice grounds you in the present moment and can stop you from feeling anxious and stressed; it can be particularly beneficial for busy people.

Duration: a few minutes

1. Prop yourself up in bed, sit in a comfortable chair or lie on the floor. Make yourself comfortable, ensuring that your back is supported if you are in bed or sitting in a chair. You may wish to close your eyes.

2. Breathe in and out a few times. Settle your attention on your breath. Imagine the breath moving in and out like the waves of an ocean, calmly and evenly.

3. Breathe in and out, steadily allowing the natural breath to flow. Focusing on the breath, in and out. Continue breathing.

4. If thoughts come, let them go and guide your awareness back to the breath. In and out. Continue to move through your mindful minutes, until you feel a sense of settling. Each breath is a unit of its own. One in, one out, coming, going, flowing ...

5. Complete this practice with a big stretch and then return to the day ahead.

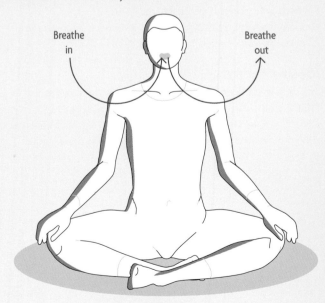

Breathe in

Breathe out

Every Breath You Take

People who don't practise mindfulness, or yoga, often have a higher rate of breaths per minute because they are living in a stressed state, or are more likely to move into this state as an automatic response.

As time moves on, you will most probably discover that your breathing rate slows down and that your breathing deepens like that of a baby. Have you ever watched a little newborn baby and seen how its whole chest fills up with air, a bit like a balloon? You could try putting one hand on your chest and the other hand on your abdomen to see how your breathing evolves, but no pressure.

What to Write in Your Mindfulness Journal

Reflect on your Mindful Minute sessions immediately after you have experienced them. While things are still fresh in your mind and body, ask yourself the following questions:

- How was the quality of the breath? Was it even, uneven, deep or short?
- What emotions did you experience during the session/practice?
- Were you able to use the breath as an anchor to move away from your thoughts during the minute?
- Has the practice become smoother and more natural as the days have moved on?
- What was particularly challenging?
- Does the Mindful Minute continue to be the same or change each time you return to the practice?

Closing Thoughts

This second week will give you a valuable calming tool in the form of the Mindful Minute, and it is a fantastic way to start the day because it reboots your mind into a peaceful state. Don't forget, you can use the Mindful Minute whenever you feel overwhelmed. The breath is always there to soothe you.

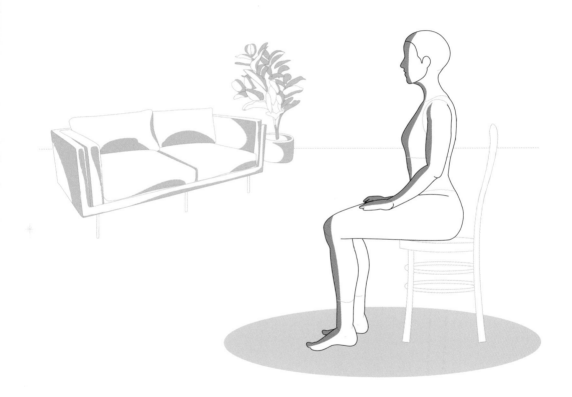

Week Three: Mindful Breathing and Sitting with Your Thoughts

In week three, you are going to combine your knowledge of working with the breath, the body and the mind. This week is focused on mindfulness and breathing, but with the added element of briefly looking at our thoughts, before letting them go.

Breathing is something we can consciously control but it also happens by itself, which makes it a wonderful tool for practising mindful awareness. Mindful breathing teaches us to remain focused in the present moment while simultaneously attempting to address thoughts that arise and allowing them to pass, whether they be negative (see NATs, page 100), pleasant or neutral.

The Benefits of Mindful Breathing and Sitting with Your Thoughts

- Calms the mind and boosts mental wellbeing
- Reduces the stress response ("fight or flight") in the body
- Lowers the heart rate and blood pressure
- Floods the body with oxygen
- Prevents overthinking and reduces NATs

Challenges for This Week

When people start any mindful breath practice, they often tend to control the breath rather than allowing it to happen naturally; you may have experienced this challenge during week two with the Mindful Minute.

Even if your breathing is steady and even, this exercise can raise another challenge – that of the racing thoughts (or what Buddhists call "the monkey mind"). Your thoughts will surface in many ways but probably mostly about the exercise itself: "My neck feels stiff", "Am I doing this properly?" and "This is boring" may be some of your automatic mental responses. Bigger thoughts about your life may also creep in. Whatever the mind clutter, the approach this week is for you to look at your thoughts as if you are an external observer. Consider your thoughts as events of the mind that are not necessarily true or false. Your thoughts are not facts, they are only events; see if you can separate yourself from your mental chatter.

In order to achieve this position of detachment, you are going to use your breath as your anchor. Whenever you find your mind wandering come back to the breath.

Mental Images for Thought Control

A visualization in your mind's eye can be a helpful way to let go of any thoughts that arise during this week's breath and thought meditation. Perhaps try out these visualizations before you do the main exercise of Sitting with Your Thoughts?

Close your eyes and connect to each technique in turn.

- Imagine you are holding a bunch of balloons. Write any thoughts that arise in your mind onto them (one thought per balloon). Read each thought, then let go of the balloon and watch it rise up into the sky. Repeat this process with all your thoughts and balloons.
- If you have more of an affinity to water, imagine standing on a bridge, seeing leaves flow by under you in the water below. The leaves are your thoughts, floating gently away from you.
- If you feel playful, you could imagine blowing soap bubbles into the air: each bubble contains a thought, an insight; it floats away and then bursts. Gone!

Use your favourite of these three techniques during the week to help you acknowledge and then let go of your thoughts.

Week Three Practice: Sitting with Your Thoughts (2)

By observing your thoughts, you create distance from them, helping you to be less affected by the mind's clutter. In essence, through this practice you can learn to manage the mind's chatter and find points of stillness. As with the other meditations, you may wish to record the instructions and play them back to follow during your daily practice throughout this week.

Duration: 10–15 minutes

1. Go to your allocated meditation place and find a comfortable position; this can be sitting in a chair or lying on the ground/bed.

2. Focus on being really grounded. If you are sitting on a chair, feel your feet firmly on the floor (or on a footstool) and your sitting bones on the chair. If you are lying on your bed, feel your body sinking and relaxing into the mattress; if on the floor, feel your head, shoulders, hips, legs and heels firmly connecting to your yoga mat. You are solid, stable, connected to the Earth.

3. Gently close your eyes if that feels appropriate for you. Now, start to focus on your breathing. Bring your awareness to your breath. Breathe naturally, finding your own rhythm. Breathe in and out. Listen to the soft, soothing sound of your breath. Breathe in and out. Your breath is your anchor of attention.

4. When you experience a sense of settling or even calmness, bring your awareness to your body, the space you are taking up. You may notice the points of connection with the floor again, or the bed, or feel a sensation on your skin. Let your attention move around your body and then bring it back to the breath. Your breath is your focus, breathing in and out.

5. Now, just keep breathing, and perhaps notice information arising in your awareness – it could be single words, sentences, feelings, sensations, colours or shapes. When you become aware of something, simply notice it and let it pass by, like a bird flying into the sky and out of your mind. Or you may prefer to use another visualization to attend to your thoughts: the balloons, the leaves under the bridge or the soap bubbles (see page 261). You know what works best for you. Choose a mental image to help you let your thoughts drift away. Yes, give your thoughts space, but then let them go without needing to understand or change anything. Remember, thoughts are not facts, they do not define you.

6. Breathe, connect with the breath as you let any negative thoughts or emotions come and go.

7. After a while, when information starts to repeat itself or stops, return to your breathing as your anchor of awareness, until you decide to end this meditation.

8. When you are ready, take a few deep breaths, stretch, open your eyes and gently reconnect to being fully alert, ready to continue with the rest of the day.

What to Write in Your Mindfulness Journal

Reflect on the sessions immediately after you have experienced them. While things are still fresh in your mind and body, ask yourself the following questions:

- What was the quality of your breath during this practice? Was it even and smooth, or short and shallow?
- Did you find it easy to fall into a natural rhythm of breath?
- How did the breathing make your body feel?
- What kind of thoughts came up during this practice?
- Was it easy to let these thoughts go?
- Did the thoughts affect your breathing or breath awareness?
- What triggered real enthusiasm during the session/practice?
- What was particularly challenging? Does it continue to be the same or change each time you return to it during this breathing practice?

Closing Thoughts

The breath creates space in your mind, it creates a stillness where you can be present and realize that your thoughts are not you – they come and go. Mindful breathing can foster a new way to respond to NATs. Now you have the choice, and the tools, to acknowledge negative thoughts and let them go.

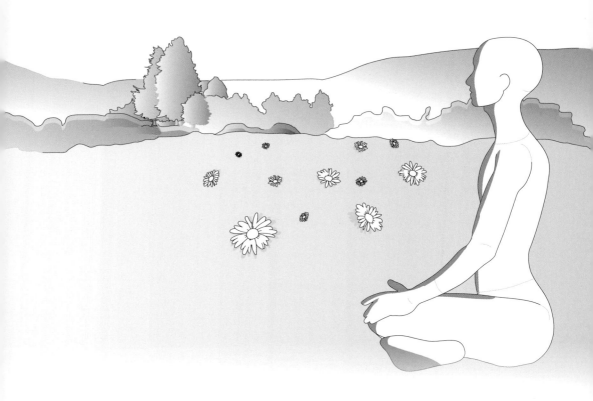

Week Four: Mindful Movement

In week four you are going to focus on the quality of movement as a mindfulness practice. Mindful movement is a powerful tool for staying present because it involves awareness and acceptance of our current experience; it invites us to embrace both negative and positive feelings and sensations in the body. As we inhabit our body, mindful movement can help us connect deeply to any emotions and sensations we are presently experiencing in our "home" and understand them more profoundly. We listen by adjusting slowly, mindfully, into each movement. We become aware of the quality of our movements and the breath with each posture. This state of active and open attention to the present moment is at the heart of all of our mindfulness practices.

Mindful movement, however, is very different from any rigorous physical exercise. It works from the inside of your body. Its movements are based within your natural range of motion; they may be enjoyable, tiny gentle stretches and movements with a period of holding, during which you can explore your physical sensations and your reactions to them more fully. You may experience a sense of lightness or even inner delight. It is a moment of deep connection within you.

This practice of moving mindfully could just be gently lifting your arms, stretching your hands or fingers or nodding your head. You may find that stroking up and down the sides of your legs is comforting. Are you ready to experiment? If mindful movement entices you, consider exploring yoga, Pilates or Tai Chi. You may even start paying attention when going for a walk, cleaning your windows or doing some gardening. Whatever the movement, it will help strengthen your capacity to embrace both the beauty and challenges of life.

Mindful movement may be a step toward wholeness, helping you to accept yourself more deeply. This week you may move a step closer to learning to listen to, accept and love your wonderful body and appreciate all that it does for you.

The Benefits of Mindful Movement

- Helps us to listen to our bodies and discover new aspects about movement
- Fosters an acceptance, and self-love, of our bodies whatever their ability, size and shape
- Promotes a sense of calm and greater clarity in thinking
- May help to increase cardiovascular activity and releases tension
- May help us stop rushing, slow down and reduce the stress response

Challenges for This Week

Hurrying is a major reason why many of us are not fully present in daily life. It becomes almost impossible to pay attention when rushing, which can make us more susceptible to injury. By slowing down and becoming aware, we can notice our patterns of moving body and mind.

Try to slow down this week. It is important to tune into the body's language and never to strain or go further than the body will allow. Listen to the "small voice" within that tells you to stop. Let yourself be surprised by how wonderful a gentle movement session can make you feel: free and at ease!

As a saying goes: the body is your temple and you are the deity in it. The temple protects you, shelters you, serves you. By practising in an embodied way, we free ourselves from the habits of doing, seeing and feeling things in autopilot mode, and we begin to open the door to new ways of being.

Week Four Practice: Simple Sun Salutation

As you discovered in A Mindful Day, the Sun Salutation is traditionally practised at sunrise to awaken the mind, body and spirit to the day ahead. The gentle series of stretches will help you connect with your body and feel at one with yourself and the world around you.

Following the instructions on pages 54–59, complete one whole round of the Simple Sun Salutation. Over the week, build up your stamina to a maximum of five rounds. You will notice that some days you are more flexible (and stronger) than others, which is fine. What is important is to move with the breath and always within your comfortable range.

Week Four Practice: Spinal Rotation

The spine supports the body and without it you could not stand upright. The spine also protects the spinal cord (the column of nerves that connects your brain to the rest of your body), which is why it is so important to keep your spine healthy.

From a mindfulness point of view, you can view the spine as the physical link between the body and mind. Engaging in a spinal rotation connects these two aspects, keeping you fit, mentally active and present.

Caution: Spinal rotation is an advanced practice for people who are very mobile – please only attempt this practice if you are very fit and healthy, particularly in relation to your spine.

Duration: 5–10 minutes

1. Lie on your back on a yoga mat and come into Constructive Resting Pose (CRP) by placing your feet hip-width apart and bringing your knees together to touch.

2. Let your arms rest on the mat in a T-shape, away from your body, with your palms facing upward. If it feels comfortable, you can bring both hands to your belly and let them sit gently as you rest in CRP.

3. Make any minor movements you need to feel comfortable. Feel your shoulders connecting with the Earth evenly and make sure your neck is not twisting to one side.

4. Now, connect to your breath. Breathe in and out, find your natural rhythm. If your hands are on your belly, feel the stomach rise with every inhale and lower with every exhale. Breathe. Stay in CRP for as long as you like. Then, when you feel ready, move on to the next step to begin the spinal rotation.

5. Bring your feet and knees together. Move your arms into a V-shape if they are not already in this position.

6. Inhale and as you exhale let your knees drop to the right, creating a twist in your spine. (If your knees don't reach the floor that's fine – listen to your body. You could, if you wish, let the knees drop onto a pillow that you position at your side.) Breathe. Toward the end of the movement, turn your head to the left (the opposite direction to your knees). If this neck movement is uncomfortable, turn the head to look right (the same direction as your knees).

7. Stay in this spinal rotation position for a few breaths. When you are ready, inhale and on the exhale bring the knees back to the centre. Take any movement you need to come back to the neutral starting position.

8. When you are ready, inhale and on the exhale let the knees fall to the left, again let the head turn to the right if this feels good for you. Breathe into the twist.

9. Repeat this spinal rotation (left and right) three times. Sink deeper into the twist with each cycle and use the breath to help you focus and relax. Breathing in and out, steadily, naturally.

10. After your last cycle, bring the body back to CRP for a moment, then gently bring both knees to the chest – but don't hug them right into your breastbone. Release your legs and have a full body stretch, taking a deep breath, pause, then let everything go – relax, feel your body connecting to the mat.

11. When you are ready, roll onto your favourite side and slowly use your hands to push yourself up to a seated position and come to standing carefully.

12. Stand in Mountain Pose (see page 122), feel your feet rooted to the ground. Take a few deep breaths to end the practice.

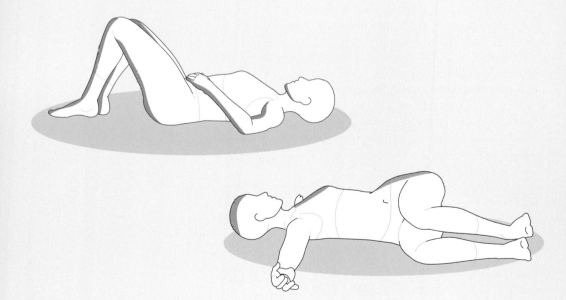

Week Four Practice: Mindful Walking (2)

A walking meditation can be done either inside or outside. Aim to walk mindfully for about ten minutes initially, and expand it gradually to 20 minutes, should you wish to do so. If you can, turn off your mobile phone or at least put it on silent to help you fully connect to this mindful practice.

Duration: 10–20 minutes

1. First, take a stance, really feeling connected to the Earth, with your feet hip-width apart and very solidly rooted to the ground. Before you start walking, really observe the area you are intending to walk in, always keeping your eyes open and looking straight ahead, not down. Very slowly start to lift your right foot from the ground. Notice the heel peeling off the ground and your weight simultaneously shifting into the left leg and foot.

2. After having peeled the right heel off, observe how you are moving it forward ever so slowly, shifting the foot and then gently placing it down exactly one step ahead.

3. While you are placing the right foot down, observe the left heel beginning to peel off the ground and your weight shifting back into the right leg. You may feel slightly "wobbly" at first, as you have slowed down the pace so much. What can be helpful is imagining making real footprints into the ground (like walking on a sandy beach). Your awareness will be fully occupied with the "lifting, shifting and placing" of each footstep, and with mindfully observing how your weight shifts from left to right, and back again.

4. When you have found your natural (and slower) walking pace, start to focus on your environment. Take in anything that your eyes can see – grass, trees, flowers, animals, clouds, stones. Also listen to the sounds around you – what can you hear?

5. Now focus on the air. Is it hot, cool, sharp, warm? How does the air make your body feel? If you are walking outside, meander slowly and continue on your chosen path being present and in the moment.

6. If you are walking inside, or in a smaller space, when you have done ten steps in one direction, take your time turning around. Observe with curiosity how your hips swirl round very gradually. Before starting your next set of steps, stand once again, mindfully rooted to the ground, just breathing.

What to Write in Your Mindfulness Journal

Reflect on your mindful movement sessions immediately after you have experienced them. While things are still fresh in your mind and body, ask yourself the following questions:

- How did your body feel during your mindful movement practice? Were any particular areas tight or sore? Or did the mindful movement feel natural at all?
- What was your reaction at first to your body? Did this emotional response change by the end of the practice?
- Did you have any expectations of your body before the mindful movement?
- What have you learnt about your body?
- Has your relationship with your body changed in any way?
- Did you listen to your body? What was it trying to tell you?

Go with the Flow

You may wish to start your day with a few Sun Salutations (see page 54) or a Spinal Rotation (see page 268), and end it with the walking meditation. Or, you may prefer to start the day with a walking meditation and end with the Sun Salutation or a Spinal Rotation – go with what works best for you.

Closing Thoughts

It is time to stop comparing your body with those of others. Embrace your body with all of its quirks, strengths and weaknesses. Move with grace and wonder; your body is the only one you have so mindfully learn to embrace it with kindness and gratitude.

Week Five: The Three-step Breathing Space

You may have experienced some challenges as you attempted to fit in longer daily meditation practices over the previous four weeks. Whatever your experience, well done for having tried and for giving it your best. As the saying goes, Rome was not built in a day. Remember, you will have the rest of your life to practise.

I do hope you have started to feel some benefits from practising the Body Scan, mindful breathing, sitting with your thoughts and mindful movement in one form or another. Even if you have just managed to eat a few spoonfuls of your breakfast or brushed your teeth mindfully, excellent, well done, bravo!

The Three-step Breathing Space is the signature practice of MBCT. It can be so powerful that it may help you to switch off the "fight or flight" mode (sympathetic nervous system) and put the body into a relaxed state (parasympathetic nervous system) with all of the benefits this brings.

The Benefits of the Three-step Breathing Space

- Reduces stress and can stop the stress loop. The body learns not to overreact to a perceived threat, which isn't a real threat at all.
- Creates a new insight – forms a calmer way to respond to potential triggers in the future.
- It may even boost the immune system because it is not constantly under pressure with stress.
- It may reduce the likelihood of developing auto-immune disorders such as chronic fatigue and lupus, to name two.
- It may promote better sleep and digestion.
- Improves attention span and mental focus.
- Reduces the risk of developing chronic illness associated with stress such as heart disease, obesity, depression and anxiety, asthma, headaches, gastrointestinal problems and Alzheimer's disease.

Challenges for This Week

When you meditate and do this week's practice, you may find yourself in a challenging life situation, experience negative automatic thoughts or a negative mood. By using this tool, you can focus and anchor your awareness away from your thoughts and choose not to engage with them.

Recognizing that the same patterns of thought(s) may recur again and again can help us to stand back from them and not interact with them during the meditation. You learned this skill in week three with the Sitting with Your Thoughts exercise (and with other practices you may have experimented with in this book). If you find it difficult to detach from your thoughts while doing the Three-step Breathing Space exercise maybe revisit Sitting with Your Thoughts (see page 262) once or twice before re-engaging with this week's practice.

If you find that negative thought patterns persist, you can choose to work with them cognitively, with an attitude of investigation, curiosity and kindness. I recommend writing these thoughts in your journal after the meditation. This way you will remain a calm observer during the practice, as if you are standing behind a waterfall, noticing what the mind brings up but knowing deeply that you are not your thoughts and that they will be impermanent.

See your thoughts as coming, going, taking a pause and possibly recurring. This way of standing back involves seeing thoughts and feelings from the perspective of the interested observer or compassionate witness.

You may also notice sounds as you sit or stand (this practice can be done in whatever posture you choose). Again, notice when they arise and try to simply hear the sounds rather than listen and judge. Then, like thoughts, let them go and refocus on the breath and your awareness.

Week Five Practice: Three-step Breathing Space (2)

This practice is an adapted version of the one you encountered in A Mindful Day (see page 68). For this week, I'm going to ask you to do the exercise at home. Kindly practise it when you feel it is convenient for you. There is no right or wrong length of time to practise, just do what you sense is right for you on any given day.

Before you begin this practice, you may find it helpful to visualize the shape of an hourglass with the letter "A" for Awareness at the top of the hourglass, the letter "G" for Gathering at the narrow part of the hourglass and the letter "E" for Expanding at the bottom of the hourglass. This image and the acronym AGE will help you keep track of the three-step sequence.

Duration: 3–5 minutes

1. **Awareness**: Settle into a comfortable position. Roll your shoulders to open your heart area. Now ask yourself: "What am I thinking, feeling or sensing in my body right now?" Don't censor your answers, don't engage with the thoughts, merely observe.

2. **Gathering**: Now, engage in mindful breathing. The breath is your anchor. Breathe in and out slowly, evenly. Practise at least five rounds of mindful in-and out-breathing to settle yourself further and feel at ease. If thoughts come, let them pass. Refocus on the breath.

3. **Expanding**: Get a sense of your body and the space it takes up as a whole, as if you were using a pencil and were drawing a line around the outer edges of your body. Say to yourself, "This is my space. This is me and I am strong." Feel your feet deeply grounded, almost as if roots are growing out of the soles of your feet and into the floor. Now visualize an image of strength: a tree, a mountain or the calm sea. Use this mental focus to occupy your mind and take it away from thought.

4. If you are doing a shorter three-minute practice, you can choose to end the meditation here with a few deep breaths. If you are engaging in a longer practice, you can go back to the beginning and progress through steps 1–3 again: Awareness, Gathering, Expanding. Do as many cycles of the sequence as feels comfortable within your set time.

What to Write in Your Mindfulness Journal

Reflect on this meditation immediately after your practice. While things are still fresh in your mind, ask yourself the following questions:

- Was it easy or challenging to be present for this length of time?
- What did you find helpful about this practice? Was anything difficult?
- Did any thoughts come up? How did you deal with them this time?
- Did you feel any sense that time stretched or contracted – meaning a short period felt much longer or a longer period felt shorter? What do you think about this experience?
- How did your body feel physically? Did your heartbeat and breathing seem settled? Did you feel comfortable and at ease?
- How has this practice changed as the days have progressed?

Closing Thoughts

There is no right or wrong way to meditate mindfully. Everyone's experience will be different. I can guide you through the practice, but there is only your way of doing this at this moment, and it will change. Nothing is permanent. The invitation is to trust that sooner or later sitting with your awareness, and connecting with the breath and body, will slowly reduce your stress levels and lead to a calmer way of being.

Week Six: A Day of Living Mindfully

We are embarking on the last week of this course, I hope that you now feel more
confident in your mindfulness practice and have found some favourite techniques.
You are probably already using some of these methods automatically throughout
your day, and mindfulness may have become much more familiar to you.

This final week aims to foster your awareness further and apply the principles you
are already using to other activities in your day. Perhaps you have already tried
"mindful eating" during the Raisin Exercise (see page 64) or engaged in a mindful
morning walk. Take a moment right now to quickly write a list in your journal
of the ways you have come to practise mindfulness during the day. Once you've
written the list come back to this page.

Mindfulness in Action

Look at your list. Do you tend to cram your mindful activities into the morning or
do you leave your mindfulness practice until the evening, when you feel exhausted
and are beginning to fall asleep? Nobody is perfect and this is not a criticism, we
can all be more mindful during our day.

Can you think of any times in the day when you could perhaps slot in a few more
moments of mindfulness? Here are some examples: brushing your teeth, having a
shower, shaving, getting dressed, doing the washing up, walking to the car, getting
into a car or onto a bus, before eating, walking the dog, getting ready for bed. Can
you think of any more moments?

Week Six Practice: Mindfulness Wheel

This exercise will help you create your ideal mindful day. You might like to create different Mindfulness Wheels for the weekend, holidays or any other special types of days.

Duration: 5–10 minutes

1. Draw a circle and split it into four sections, Divide these quarters again so you have eight segments in total (rather like a wheel).

2. Starting at the top of the circle, work your way around this Mindfulness Wheel noting mindful practices you can do from waking up to bedtime, including a rough time for each activity. For example:

Segment one: 7.30am. Wake up. Short mental gratitude list.
Segment two: 7.45am. Brush teeth mindfully.
Segment three: 7.55am. Walking meditation.
Segment four: 11.30am. Mindful Minute before meeting.
And so on ...

Depending on your circumstances, your own ideal mindfulness day may look very different to my suggestions! However you approach this week, having your mindfulness practices in place will help you to deal with stressful situations. This wheel gives you a framework, it is not set in stone and you can adapt your Mindfulness Wheel to suit you.

Mindfulness Throughout the Day

Here are some more tips to help you engage further in mindfulness during your day. You may also like to re-read A Mindful Day (see page 46).

- When you wake up in the morning, bring your attention to your breathing. Observe five mindful breaths before getting out of bed.
- Whenever you hear a phone ring, or a bird sing, a train pass, or an alarm, use that sound like a bell of mindfulness. Really listen, feeling present and awake.
- Throughout the day use a few moments to bring your attention to your breathing. You can practise a Mindful Minute (see page 257).
- Whenever you eat or drink something, do so with your full awareness. Pay attention as you eat; eating is not an automatic process but a physical experience to be enjoyed.
- Pay attention to your body while you are walking or standing. Notice your posture, notice your speed of movement. Are you rushing?
- Bring awareness to your conversations, listen to the other person. Engage.
- If you are waiting in a queue, bring your attention to the rising and falling of your abdomen.
- Before going to sleep, write a gratitude list in your Gratitude Journal (see page 74). Look over the pages and see how you have developed and progressed on your journey.

And Finally ...

Once you have completed the six-week course, the invitation is to continue practising for the rest of your life. Make mindfulness part of your daily routine, commit to living in the now, to not letting negative thoughts push you into the stress response. Try to be mindful for as many moments of the day as you remember, and be kind to yourself, be patient and compassionate. You have just started a journey; may it be a long and fruitful one. You have been offered a lot of knowledge of how to engage with people (and animals) with kindness and awareness.

To support your continuing mindfulness journey, you'll find a variety of useful information in the Resources section of the book, including recommended websites, blogs and apps that will help you explore mindfulness further (see page 282), guidance about what to look for on a mindfulness retreat (see page 286) and – if you feel inspired to do so – advice about how to train as a mindfulness teacher so you can help others (see page 288).

Enjoy being present with all the wonderful rewards this will bring both physically, mentally and spiritually.

6
RESOURCES

Useful Mindfulness Websites, Blogs and Apps

These resources are not a comprehensive list, but they will guide you in the right direction should you wish to explore mindfulness further or train to become a teacher.

Suggested Websites

aheadforwork.com
Created by author and mindfulness coach Juliet Adams, A Head For Work is an extensive resource relating to all aspects of mindfulness.

bemindfulonline.com
A mindfulness course to reduce anxiety, depression and stress.

chrisgermer.com
Dr Chris Germer is the co-developer of the Mindful Self Compassion (MSC) training programme; his site is packed with resources. The free meditations include both digital downloads and written instructions.

entermindfulness.com
The website for Dr Patrizia Collard's mindfulness workshops.

mentalhealth.org.uk
A wealth of resources relating to mental wellbeing from the UK's Mental Health Foundation.

mindful.org
The website for the US magazine *Mindful*. You don't have to subscribe to the magazine to access the site's free content.

mindfulnessforteens.com
Written by Dr Dzung Vo, a paediatrician and author, the site is packed with free mindfulness MP3 downloads that teens can save onto their gadgets and covers topics like "Help, I'm stressed about going back to school" and "Mindfulness for young people".

oxfordmindfulness.org
The University of Oxford Mindfulness Centre offers free weekly mindfulness sessions and the latest mindfulness research and news.

pvfhk.org
The Asian Institute of Applied Buddhism (AIAB) often hosts free online Days of Mindfulness and other meditation events.

self-compassion.org
All-in-one resource for self-compassion and mindfulness from Dr Kristin Neff, the co-creator of the Center for Mindful Self-Compassion with Dr Chris Germer.

Suggested Blogs

artofmindfulness.org

Artist Wendy Ann Greenhalgh blogs about mindfulness and creativity and offers a free three-week mindfulness art course *Stop Look Breath Create*.

theblissfulmind.com

This blog's main aim is to help you reduce burnout and overwhelm. Run by mindset coach Catherine Beard, this site is a fantastic hub for mindfulness.

franticworld.com/blog

Award-winning mindfulness pioneer and author Dr Danny Penman writes a blog full of clarity and authority, which provides trusted information on all aspects of mindfulness.

pocketmindfulness.com

A popular mindfulness blog by author Alfred James, full of practices, mindfulness features and suggestions for reading.

practicalmeditation.co.uk

Founded by a barrister and meditation teacher Gillian Higgins, this blog is easy to navigate and is full of mindfulness techniques to download (for free) that can be used at home and in the workplace.

simplemindfulness.com

Author Paige Oldham describes her blog as providing "simple steps to a simple life". She provides articles about mindfulness and health, relationship and finances.

tinybuddha.com

Author Lori Deschene, who hosts Tiny Buddha, offers a range of information about how to incorporate mindfulness into all areas of your life.

zenhabits.net

A no-frills blog hosted by writer and Zen expert Leo Babauta. Click on "archives" for the free material.

Suggested Mindfulness Apps

Apps can be a fantastic way to connect with daily mindfulness techniques. Calm and Headspace are two popular apps, but there are thousands on the market. Many are by subscription although some like Insight Timer are free.

Aura: Mindfulness, Sleep, Meditation.
If you like nature sounds opt for this choice, Aura also offers thousands of meditations for stress, anxiety and sleep plus a gratitude journal.

Breethe: Calm Meditation Tracks and Sleep Sounds
The app includes breathing practices and tips for coping with overwhelm as well as guided meditations to help you sleep better.

Buddhify: Meditation on the Go
If you like the Mindfulness Wheel (see page 277) then this app is for you; the sessions are offered in a similar format and range from 4- to 30-minutes long.

Calm: Manage Your Stress with Calm
Probably one of the most popular mindfulness apps, Calm aims to help you unwind, sleep better and has the bonus of music and a mood check-in feature.

Headspace: Meditation and Sleep Made Simple
Another well-known meditation app, Headspace offers meditation and mindfulness sessions that come in three-, five- or ten-minute blocks.

Insight Timer: Free App for Sleep, Anxiety and Stress
This app boasts around 20,000 free meditations, ideal if you are on a budget and don't want to pay an annual subscription fee.

Mindfulness: Finding Peace in a Frantic World
Originally developed as a research project at Oxford University, this app contains meditations from Dr Danny Penman's bestselling book *Mindfulness* plus an eight-week course.

Minding
This award-winning mindfulness app by Monty Cholmeley is a step-by-step, easy-going guide to mindfulness meditation.

MyLife Meditation: Stop. Breathe. Think.
This app helps you to find a quiet place within and recommends meditations and mindfulness practices based on your own emotional rating.

Simple Habit: The meditation app for busy people
This app is a good choice if you want to focus your mindfulness on a specific area like post-argument mindfulness, a stress-free work commute or a mindfulness practice to start (or end) your day.

Stop, Breathe & Think Kids: Helps Kids Discover the Superpower of Quiet
The children's version of the MyLife app (see above). This app for 5–10 year olds aims to promote a sense of calm, better sleep and help children to deal with negative emotions.

APPS AND LOGGING OFF

Apps are one of the most important developments within the mindfulness (and meditation) field. Before mindfulness apps, there was a stigma that went with meditators; telling people that you meditated was another way of saying that there was something wrong.

Apps may promise a mindfulness coach on your phone, but really this is not the case. We need to remember that learning mindfulness with an app is a one-way experience; you hear the guidance and practise the meditation and then that's it. You don't get any interaction with a teacher, which means if you have any questions, for the most part, you're on your own.

Without having a teacher there to help guide you through the experience it might be unpleasant or at times even dangerous. That said, some apps do offer email support from teachers; even so, if you suffer from any mental-health problems do opt instead to learn mindfulness face-to-face with an experienced practitioner.

The other downside about apps is that they are connected to your phone, which can be a great source of stress and anxiety for many people; the technology can stop us from being present in the moment. If you know that you have difficulty switching off from checking your messages, emails and so on, then perhaps you may be better using mindfulness downloads on your iPad or laptop (rather than a mobile app) – or at least create some boundaries around your app use and your phone.

For example, after doing a mindfulness practice using an app, do not check your messages or surf the net for a set period of time. Alternatively, use an app just before bedtime and turn your phone off immediately after your practice – or switch to silent mode. This way, you will not be interacting with technology and undoing all the good work of your mindfulness practice.

Mindfulness Retreats

Prolonged periods of mindfulness can provide you with opportunities for greater insight into the mind-body complex and the meditations themselves. Ideally, you might undertake a silent retreat of three to five days (or more) once or twice a year.

Retreats are not simply extensions of your daily practice, they are not just "more of the same". A retreat can help your mindfulness experience to become more profound thanks to the formal, and guided, practice over several consecutive days.

The arising and ending of sensations, emotions and thoughts over a prolonged period can have deep potential for experience and insight. Furthermore, a retreat gives you the opportunity to experience joy and peacefulness but also allows unfinished business to arise and, hopefully, will teach you to deal with such challenges in a meditative way.

Many retreats are run as a group activity, which aims to enrich and encourage both teachers and participants who might have become stuck and limited in their meditation and want to adapt new ideas into their practice.

The retreat usually starts with a check on how your mindfulness practice is working for you at present. You will be supported to develop an understanding of any obstacles and then think afresh as to what will continue to have impact and meaning for you.

The teacher will guide you through the group meditations and help you to examine the true meanings of compassion and acceptance in a non-judgemental way. A retreat always embraces periods of complete silence too, but there should be times for sharing and connecting with other participants – unless it's a silent retreat!

Depending on the focus, a retreat's format usually includes a mix of guided meditation, solo practice, opportunities for one-to-one time with the teacher and mindful movement including walking meditation. After the retreat, you should return home refreshed with some new techniques to incorporate into your mindfulness practice.

Aims of a Retreat

- Deepen your personal mindfulness practice
- Embody a mindful and compassionate stance toward life
- Enrich and sustain mindful movement
- Make space for simply being and find new space for inspiration

Retreat Guidelines

What to check before you book any retreat:

- **The cost**: How much is the retreat? When does this sum need to be paid?
- **What the price includes**: How many mindfulness sessions will there be? Does the price include accommodation and/or transport to and from the station/airport?
- **Type of accommodation**: Will you be sharing a room or dorm? Is there a single person supplement? Are the rooms en-suite?
- **Food:** What kind of food is provided ? Can they accommodate dietary requests?
- **Rules**: Are there any special rules? Many retreats (especially if at a Buddhist monastery) ask you not to bring alcohol, to avoid smoking and some even ban coffee. Check before you book.
- **Daily tasks**: Some retreats may ask you to take part in daily tasks to help with the running of the centre (like washing dishes or cooking). If you prefer a "hotel" experience for your accommodation, then book a mindfulness retreat with one of the more upmarket operators rather than a Buddhist centre.
- **Expectations**: Check the aim of the retreat matches your expectations. Ask what is the retreat's focus. Even so, try to go with an open mind because it will help you to gain more out of the experience.

Training to Become a Mindfulness Teacher

You may have found your mindfulness journey so inspiring that you wish to train as a teacher. There are many courses available: online, residential, community education and so on. Whatever course you take, make sure that it meets your expectations and find out which organization provides the course's accreditation.

In the UK, the British Association for Mindfulness-based Approaches (BAMBA; bamba.org.uk) offers mindfulness training via a hub of affiliated organizations and runs a teacher register. Dr Patrizia Collard's own teacher training, Enter Mindfulness (entermindfulness.com), runs small-number courses to enable people who have no prior teaching experience to flourish and be supported in-depth.

In the US, the Center for Mindfulness (CFM; umassmemorialhealthcare.org) offers eight-week mindfulness teacher training courses as well as access to a global mindfulness community, while Mindful Schools (Mindfulschools.org), based in California, provides mindfulness training in adults to use with young people in schools.

As mindfulness trainers, you should endeavour to embody the foundations of mindfulness within yourself and your students:

- **Patience**: Practise being calm even when stress is triggering the "fight or flight" response.
- **Non-judgement and acceptance**: Attempt as best as you can to bring kindness and compassion to life's challenges.
- **Beginner's mind**: Bring curiosity to the mindfulness adventure of experimenting with doing things differently (like sitting with discomfort for a little and seeing whether anything shifts of its own accord).
- **Trust**: Mindfulness meditation and compassion techniques have been around for thousands of years. Trust that mindfulness works to help people manage difficult life situations.
- **Kindness**: Bring an attitude of gentleness to the process. Treat yourself, and your students, as you would treat a vulnerable child or animal companion.
- **Non-striving**: There is no medal to be won, nor riches or fame. You are doing this because you hope to experience more peace and tranquillity in your life (and teach help others to access this state too).

Whatever you decide, permit yourself to freely float into the experience without any attachment to an outcome or insight. Just "be" for the sake of being.

Bibliography

Adams, Juliet, *Intention Matters: The science of creating the life you want* (Intentional Creations, 2019).

Atkinson, Karen, *Compassionate Mindful Inquiry in Therapeutic Practice: A Practical Guide for Mindfulness Teachers, Yoga Teachers and Allied Health Professionals* (Singing Dragon, 2020).

Bien, Thomas and **Bien, Beverly**, *Mindful Recovery: A Spiritual Path to Healing from Addiction* (John Wiley, 2002).

Burch, Vidyamala and **Penman, Danny**, *Mindfulness for Health* (Piatkus, 2013).

Cayoun, Bruno A, *Mindfulness-Integrated CBT for Well-Being and Personal Growth* (John Wiley, 2015).

Chaskalson, Michael and **Reitz, Megan**, *Mind Time: How 10 Mindful Minutes Can Enhance Your Work, Health and Happiness* (Thorsons, 2018).

Collard, Patrizia, *The Mindfulness Bible: The Complete Guide to Living in the Moment* (Octopus, 2015).

Feldman, Christina, *Meditation: Plain and Simple* (Element Books, 2004).

Feldman, Christina and **Kuyken, Willem**, *Mindfulness: Ancient Wisdom Meets Modern Psychology* (Guilford Press, 2019).

Kabat-Zinn, Jon, *Gesund durch Meditation: Das große Buch der Selbstheilung* (Fischer Taschenbuch Verlag, 2006).

Maex, Edel, *Mindfulness: Der achtsame Weg durch die Turbulenzen des Lebens* (Arbor, 2009).

Sears, Richard W, *Mindfulness: Living Through Challenges and Enriching Your Life in This Moment* (John Wiley, 2014).

Siegel, Daniel, *Mindsight: Transform Your Brain with the New Science of Kindness* (Oneworld Publications, 2010).

Siegel, Daniel, *Aware: The Science of Practice and Presence* (Scribe Publications, 2018).

Siegel, Ronald D, *The Mindfulness Solution: Everyday Practices for Everyday Problems* (Guilford Press, 2010).

Glossary

acceptance: the process of responding to difficulties with attention rather than as a thoughtless reaction

adrenaline: a hormone secreted by the adrenal glands in response to the "fight or flight" reaction

amygdalae: clusters of grey matter in the brain that form the control and response centre, switching on the "fight or flight" response and playing a major role in the expression of emotions

autopilot: the state in which we automatically respond to actions without questioning what we are doing

Body Scan: one of the main mindfulness techniques in which we scan the entire body mentally, moving the focus across the different areas one by one, in order to become fully present in the mind and body

Buddhism: a belief system that originated with Siddhartha, the Buddha, and which has had a profound influence on many aspects of mindfulness

burnout: exhaustion as a result of long-term stress

CBT (Cognitive Behavioural Therapy): a talking therapy that aims to improve mental health and treat depression

comorbidity: an overlap of different mental or physical conditions

compassion: sympathetic concern for the suffering of other people

cortisol: a stress hormone that is released during the "fight or flight" response

depression: an illness that affects how we feel, think and act; it is associated with anxiety, negative thoughts, low mood and poor self-image and can be triggered by a wide range of events

dysthymia: mild, long-term depression

endorphin: one of the body's natural feel-good chemicals that are produced in the brain and can have a painkilling and tranquillizing effect on the body

"fight or flight" response: the body's natural response to a stressful event, when it perceives a threat to its survival and prepares either to stay and fight or to flee

GAD (Generalized Anxiety Disorder): a sense of dread that something terrible is about to happen and an inability to control worries

groundedness: a feeling of mental and emotional stability when we are fully present in the body

hyperventilation: the state of breathing too fast (up to 100 times per minute), which may leave people feeling breathless

MBAT (Mindfulness-Based Attention Training): a specialized short form of mindfulness training used by the US Army

MBCT (Mindfulness-Based Cognitive Therapy): a therapy that combines mindfulness techniques with Cognitive Behavioural Therapy, to help replace with more helpful ways of thinking the negative automatic thoughts that are characteristic of depression, anxiety, stress, etc.

MBRP (Mindfulness-Based Relapse Prevention): a therapy for preventing relapse in addictive disorders by cultivating mindful awareness

MBSR (Mindfulness-Based Stress Reduction): a programme of intense mindfulness to help people cope with stress, depression, anxiety and pain

meditation: a technique that trains the mind, using mindfulness, to attain a state of calm and relaxation

Metta **meditation**: a loving-kindness, self-compassion meditation

mindful breathing: focusing on the breath, which brings feelings of calm and wellbeing and reduces stress and anxiety

mindful eating: eating and drinking with full awareness, using all our senses of taste, sight, touch, hearing and smell

mindful movement: focusing on the act of moving, which brings mind and body together

mindful walking: engaging in a walk simply for the sake of it, bringing awareness to our movements and our breathing

mindfulness: the state of being present in the "here and now" with full awareness

NATs (negative automatic thoughts): negative thinking that stops us experiencing the present moment without judgement

neuron: a cell that transmits nerve impulses to other cells in the body

neuropathway: part of a series of connected nerves along which electrical impulses travel

neuroplasticity: the capability of our brains to continue to change vigorously throughout our lives

neurotransmitter: a chemical messenger that transmits messages between neurons

OCD (Obsessive Compulsive Disorder): an anxiety disorder characterized by recurring thoughts and obsessions that people perform repetitively and are unable to control

parasympathetic nervous system: also called the "rest and digest" system – it slows down the heart rate and encourages the body to relax

PTSD (Post-Traumatic Stress Disorder): a mental-health condition triggered by a terrifying event, which causes flashbacks, nightmares and anxiety

REM (rapid eye-movement) sleep: a phase of light sleep in which deep rapid-eye movements are made

Sangha: literally, "association" or "community", often with reference to a monastic community; now used to refer in general to a shared sense of community

self-compassion: the state of applying empathy to oneself

serotonin: the body's natural "feel-good" chemical

Siddhartha: Siddhartha Gautama, the birth name of Buddha, the founder of Buddhism and "the awakened one"

Taoism: an ancient Chinese philosophy and religion based on the writings of Lao-tzu; it emphasizes "going with the flow" and following our intuition

Vedic: relating to the Sanskrit religious texts known as the Vedas

visualization: the technique of creating mental visual imagery of something – forming a picture of it in our mind

walking meditation: meditation that brings awareness to the fact that we are here now, in our gently moving body

yang: the male principle of the universe in Chinese philosophy

ying: the female principle of the universe in Chinese philosophy

yogi: someone who is proficient in yoga

Chapter Notes

Introduction

[1] "An Invitation to Unity and Love" quoted by kind permission of Georgina Hunter. Note: *prana* is the Sanskrit word for "breath", and breath is life and connects us all – the precious gift of life.

1 Awakening to Mindfulness
Mindfulness: Spirit and Science

[1] Mind and Life Institute mission statement: https://www.mindandlife.org/mission/.

[2] Jon Kabat-Zinn, "This Loving-Kindness Meditation is a Radical Act of Love"; https://www.mindful.org/this-loving-kindness-meditation-is-a-radical-act-of-love/.

[3] Author's notes from Parneet Pal's online talk at the Mindful Living Summit: Learn How to Show Up to Each Moment with Mindfulness (21 March 2020).

[4] Kahlil Gibran, from "On Pleasure", *The Prophet* (Knopf, 1968).

Why We Need Mindfulness Now More Than Ever

[1] Steve Bradt, "Wandering Mind Not a Happy Mind", *The Harvard Gazette*, 11 November 2010; https://news.harvard.edu/gazette/story/2010/11/wandering-mind-not-a-happy-mind/.

[2] Chris Germer, Kristin Neff, *Teaching the Mindful Self-Compassion Program: A Guide for Professionals* (Guilford Press, 2019).

[3] Dr Karen Neil in conversation with the author.

[4] Kahlil Gibran, from "On Love", *The Prophet* (Knopf, 1968).

Opening Up to a New Way of Living

[1] William Blake, from "Auguries of Innocence", *The Poems of William Blake* (Basil Montagu Pickering, 1874), p.145.

A Mindful Day

[1] Emily Dickinson, "LXXII", *Poems by Emily Dickinson* (Little Brown and Company, 1948).

[2] M J Ryan, *Attitudes of Gratitude* (Conari Press, 1999).

2 Relationships and Mental Wellbeing
Mindfulness for Secure Relationships

[1] James W Carson, Kimberly M Carson, Karen M Gil and Donald H Baucom, "Mindfulness-Based Relationship Enhancement." *Behaviour Therapy* 35 (2004), 471–494.

[2] Dr Donna Rockwell, "Mindfulness Meditation and Romantic Relationships"; https://www.psychalive.org/video-mindfulness-meditation-and-romantic-relationships/.

[3] Thomas Bien, *Mindful Recovery: A Spiritual Path to Healing from Addiction* (John Wiley, 2002), p.147.

[4] Kahlil Gibran, *The Prophet* (Knopf, 1968).

[5] *Walk with Me* (2017), directed by Marc J Francis and Max Pugh and starring Benedict Cumberbatch, Thich Nhat Hanh and Phap De.

[6] Monty Cholmeley in conversation with the author.

[7] Robert Burns, "A Red, Red Rose", *The Complete Works of Robert Burns* (Phillips, Sampson, and Company, 1855).

Mindfulness for Mental Wellbeing

[1] Sarah Bowen, et al. "Mindfulness-based relapse prevention for substance use disorders: a pilot efficacy trial." *Substance Abuse* 30,4 (2009), 295–305.

[2] Dr Karen Neil in conversation with the author.

[3] *Depression and Other Common Mental Disorder: Global Health Estimates*, World Health Organization (2017).

[4] David J Kearney, Kelly McDermott, Carol Malte, Michelle Martinez, Tracy L Simpson, (2012) "Association of Participation in a Mindfulness Program with Measures of PTSD, Depression and Quality of Life in a Veteran Sample." *Journal of Clinical Psychology*, 68(1) (January 2012), 101–116.

[5] Eric Lomax, *The Railway Man* (Vintage, 1995).

[6] *The Railway Man* film (2013), directed by Jonathan Teplitzky and starring Colin Firth, Nicole Kidman and Stellan Skarsgard.

[7] Elizabeth Jordan, "How do traumatised veterans experience 'mindfulness'?: A phenomenological exploration into veterans' experiences of 'mindfulness' during and after an intensive treatment programme for Post-Traumatic Stress Disorder." Dissertation. Master of Arts in Counselling and Psychotherapy, University of East London (2012).

[8] N S Scheiner, "Not 'At Ease': UK Veterans' Perceptions of the Level of Understanding of Their Psychological Difficulties Shown by the National Health Service." Doctoral Thesis. City University London, Department of Psychology (2008).

[9] Anka Vujanovic, Barbara L Niles, Ashley S Hart, Stefan K Schmertz, Carrie Potter, "Mindfulness in the Treatment of Post-Traumatic Stress Disorder Among Military Veterans." *Professional Psychology: Research and Practice* 42(1) (February 2011), 24–31.

[10] Dr B Grace Bullock, "Preventing Stress-Related Mental Decline in Soldiers", 6 February 2020, Mindful; https://www.mindful.org/preventing-stress-related-mental-decline-in-soldiers/.

[11] ibid.

[12] William Butler Yeats, "He Wishes For The Cloths of Heaven", *The Wind Among The Reeds* (John Lane: The Bodley Head, 1899), p.60.

[13] Professor Paul Gilbert, "Compassion for the Dark Side"; youtube.com/watch?v=-xSOHOfG2yE.

[14] *Broken* TV series, BBC1 (2017), directed by Ashley Pearce and Noreen Kershaw and starring Sean Bean, Adrian Dunbar and Anna Friel.

[15] Jack Kornfield, *The Art of Forgiveness, Lovingkindness and Peace* (Bantam, 2002).

3 Food and Sleep
Mindful Eating

[1] Jennifer Daubenmier, Jean Kristeller, Frederick M Hecht, Nicole Maninger, Margaret Kuwata, Kinnari Jhaveri, Robert H Lustig, Margaret Kemeny, Lori Karan, Elissa Epel, "Mindfulness Intervention for Stress Eating to Reduce Cortisol and Abdominal Fat among Overweight and Obese Women: An Exploratory Randomized Controlled Study." *Journal of Obesity* 2011 (2011): 651936.

2 Jane Goodall, *Harvest for Hope: A Guide to Mindful Eating* (Warner Books, 2005).

3 Reudiger Dahlke, *Peace Food* (Graefe und Unzer Verlag, 2011).

4 *Earthlings* (2005), directed by Shaun Monson and narrated by Joaquin Phoenix.

5 "China–Cornell–Oxford Study on Dietary, Lifestyle and Disease Mortality Characteristics in 65 Rural Chinese Counties", led by T Colin Campbell (1980s); https://www.cornell.edu/video/playlist/the-china-project-studying-the-link-between-diet-and-disease.

Sleep

1 Natalie Pennicotte-Collier, extract from talk at the Mental Health Festival 2017.

2 Peter L Franzen and Daniel J Buysse, "Sleep Disturbances and Depression: Risk Relationships for Subsequent Depression and Therapeutic Implications." *Dialogues in Clinical Neuroscience* 10(4) (2008), 473–81.

3 Goran Medic, et al. (2017), "Short- and Long-term Health Consequences of Sleep Disruption." *Nature and Science of Sleep*, 9 (2017), 151–161.

4 Amanda J Shallcross and Pallavi D Visvanathan, "Mindfulness-Based Cognitive Therapy for Insomnia" in S J Eisendrath, ed., *Mindfulness-based cognitive therapy: Innovative applications* (Springer, 2016), pp.19–29.

5 Ute Hülsheger, "A low-dose mindfulness intervention and recovery from work." *Journal of Occupational and Organizational Psychology*, 22 March 2015, Wiley Online Library; https://onlinelibrary.wiley.com/doi/abs/10.1111/joop.12115.

6 Peter Altenberg, "Friede/Peace", *Wie Ich Es Sehe* (1896) (Translated by Patrizia Collard).

4 The Gifts of Later Life
Mindful Ageing

1 Viktor Frankl, *Man's Search for Meaning* (1946; Beacon Press, 1959).

2 Edith Eger, *The Choice: Embrace the Possible* (Scribner, 2017); https://www.amazonbookreview.com/post/eb09d923-6379-400f-804d-d8a17c292168/celebrity-picks-sheryl-sandberg-s-favorite-reads-of-2017.

3 Viktor E Frankl, *The Doctor and the Soul: From Psychotherapy to Logotherapy* (Knopf, 2019), p.31.

4 Lauren F Friedman, "A Radical Experiment Tried to Make Old People Young Again — and the Results Were Astonishing", 6 April 2015, *Business Insider*; https://www.businessinsider.com/ellen-langers-reversing-aging-experiment-2015-4?r=DE&IR=T.

5 Ellen Langer, "Science of Mindlessness and Mindfulness" (29 May 2014), On Being with Krista Tippett; https://onbeing.org/programs/ellen-langer-science-of-mindlessness-and-mindfulness-nov2017/.

6 Rainer Maria Rilke, "Herbstag/Autumn Day". (Translated by Patrizia Collard).

Illness and Caregiving

1 "Difficulty and Delight" quoted by kind permission of Dr Karen Neil.

2 Maricel Tabalba, "5 Tools for Mindfulness for Caregivers", 31 January 2018, The Caregiver Space; https://thecaregiverspace.org/5-tools-for-mindfulness-for-caregivers/.

5 Your Ongoing Journey
Finding Joy and Mindful Activities

[1] Rick Hanson, "Wise Brain Bulletin", https://www.rickhanson.net/writings/wise-brain-bulletin/.

[2] Rick Hanson, "7 Facts About the Brain that Incline the Mind to Joy", https://www.rickhanson.net/seven-facts-brain-incline-mind-joy/.

[3] Rick Foster and Greg Hicks, *How We Choose to Be Happy* (TarcherPerigee, 2004), pp.151–169.

[4] Hmwe H Kyu, Victoria F Bachman, Lily T Alexander, John Everett Mumford, Ashkan Afshin, Kara Estep et al. "Physical activity and risk of breast cancer, colon cancer, diabetes, ischemic heart disease, and ischemic stroke events: systematic review and dose-response meta-analysis for the Global Burden of Disease Study 2013." *British Medical Journal* 2016, 354.

[5] Masaru Emoto, *The Hidden Messages in Water* (Simon and Schuster, 2005).

[6] Miguel Helft, "Good Vibrations : Healing Powers of Music Resonate for Researcher, Composer", 8 August 1996, *Los Angeles Times*; https://www.latimes.com/archives/la-xpm-1996-08-08-me-32296-story.html.

[7] Bethyn Casey, "Mindful Crafting", *Happiful* magazine, March 2020, p.35; https://issuu.com/happiful/docs/happiful_march_2020/37

[8] *Breathe* magazine, issue 25, spring 2020, p.74.

Index

Acknowledgements
Words of gratitude for all my wonderful helpers!

At this point I want to express my heartfelt appreciation to all the contributors who generously shared their wisdom, knowledge and insights. Opposite you will find their contact details.

Bernhard, Georgie, Karen and Monty: much gratefulness for your contributions and for sharing your inputs when this manuscript was almost finished. Your feedback helped enormously.

To Bernhard, Birgit, Georgie, Karen, Helen, Juliet, Monty and Natalie: thank you so much for sharing your specific expertise and allowing me to expand the information in this guide with it. All of you are stars, and your generosity will benefit the readers of this book. Thank you so much!

Much appreciation to my students all over the globe who allowed me to guide them and shared their experiences with me over the decades.

Contributors

Juliet Adams
aheadforwork.com
Workplace mindfulness and intention.

Birgit Beck
beck-raum-yoga.de
Yoga and MBSR.

Monty Cholmeley
entermindfulness.com and **minding.life**
Entermindfulness and Minding.

Georgie Hunter
universitality@gmail.com
Spiritual teacher and yoga teacher.

Karen E Neil
mindfulmedicine.co.uk
Mindfulness teacher and specialist pharmacist in health promotion and mental health.

Natalie Pennicotte-Collier
mindtonictherapy.com
UK sleep and mindfulness expert and performance coach.

Helen Stephenson
mindfulnessmk.com
Embodied working lies at the heart of mindfulness:mk; its founder, Helen, has more than 40 years of teaching experience and has been co-teaching with Patrizia Collard and Entermindfulness for more than a decade.

About the Author

Dr Patrizia Collard is a psychotherapist, mindfulness teacher and trainer, stress management consultant, writer and visiting professor at Rome's School of Interpersonal Cognitive Psychotherapy. Her books include *Journey into Mindfulness*, *Mindfulness-based Cognitive Behavioural Therapy for Dummies*, *Awakening the Compassionate Mind*, *The Little Book of Mindfulness*, *The Little Book of Meditation* and *The Mindfulness Bible*.

entermindfulness.com
achtsamkeitleben.at

Also Available

Godsfield Companion: Chakras
Godsfield Companion: Crystals
Godsfield Companion: Yoga